"When Philippe of the Trinity, O.C.D. went to work on what salvation in Jesus Christ means, he was pushing back against a popular rigorism alive in the French culture, a jaundiced holdover from Calvinism which stressed God's wrath and humanity's utter unlovability. This is not the Christ of the Gospels, nor is it the Christ of the Church. Rather, by reading the Tradition—St. Thomas especially—Père Philippe shows us that Jesus' Passion is not a punishment but an act of praise, an oblation in which all Christians are brought into the Father's love precisely as we are."

—Fr. David Vincent Meconi, S.J.
Catholic Studies Centre, St. Louis University

"It is wonderful to see this classic work come back into print. Though published before the Council, its central thesis about the connections between the doctrine of the Trinity and the doctrine of the Church in the love revealed in the Paschal Mystery is not only fully congruent with Conciliar teaching but also sheds light on its core insights in a way that can promote development of them now. This study is as spiritually rich as it is theologically precise, and this draws the theology of the Trinity back into the center of Christian spirituality, where it should be. Highly recommended!"

—John C. Cavadini
University of Notre Dame

"Although more than sixty years have passed since Father Philippe de la Trinité's *What Is Redemption?* first appeared in print, it remains one of the most significant books about some of the most significant things: satisfaction, sacrifice, mercy, and merit. Much like the classic *Cursus Theologicus* of the seventeenth century Discalced Carmelites of Salamanca, Father Philippe's writings are always erudite in analysis, occasionally creative in conclusion, and profoundly spiritual in orientation. Contemporary students of theology who find themselves yearning for a synthesis of sacred sources, doctrinal history, and theological principles will delight in *What Is Redemption?*"

—Fr. Cajetan Cuddy, O.P.
Dominican House of Studies Washington, D.C.

"This classic work, both accessible and profound, is mandatory reading for anyone interested in theology of the atonement. Philippe de la Trinité shows the contested legacy in Catholic thought with respect to the mystery of the Cross, and offers helpful points of orientation. Using Aquinas as a guide, he points the way toward the heart of redemption."

—Fr. Thomas Joseph White, O.P.
Pontifical University of St. Thomas

"The architects of Protestantism jettisoned the Catholic theology of vicarious satisfaction in favor of a new theology of penal substitution. They looked at the Cross and saw the Son bearing the full brunt of the Father's wrath against wicked humanity. The greatest theologians of the Catholic Church, not least St. Thomas Aquinas, saw something different. They saw the Son loving the Father with the full strength of his human and divine natures. They saw Jesus paying the debt of our sins by giving back to the Father all the love that we withhold from Him every time we sin. This little volume by Philippe de la Trinité is easily the most clarifying book I've read on this subject."

—Curtis Mitch
Associate Editor of the Ignatius Catholic Study Bible

What Is
REDEMPTION?

What Is REDEMPTION?

How Christ's Suffering Saves Us

PHILIPPE DE LA TRINITÉ
Foreword by Scott Hahn

EMMAUS
ROAD
PUBLISHING

Steubenville, Ohio
www.emmausroad.org

Emmaus Road Publishing
1468 Parkview Circle
Steubenville, Ohio 43952

© 2021 St. Paul Center.
All rights reserved. Published 2021.
Printed in the United States of America.
Third Printing 2023

Originally published in 1961 by Hawthorn Books. Translated from the
French by Anthony Armstrong, O.S.B.

Library of Congress Control Number: 2021933703
ISBN: 978-1-949013-76-4 (hard cover) / 978-1-949013-77-1 (paperback)
/ 978-1-949013-78-8 (ebook)

NIHIL OBSTAT
Daniel Duivesteijn, S.T.D.
Censor Deputatus
IMPRIMATUR
E. Morrogh Bernard
Vicarius Generalis
Westmonasterii, die xxix AUGUSTI, MCMLXI

The Nihil obstat and Imprimatur are a declaration that a book or pamphlet
is considered to be free from doctrinal or moral error. It is not implied that
those who have granted the Nihil obstat and Imprimatur agree with the
contents opinions or statements expressed.

Cover design and layout by designer Emily Demary.
Cover image: *Le Crucifix Aux Anges* (1661), Charles Le Brun,
Louvre Museum, Paris, France

CONTENTS

FOREWORD

I WAS STILL A PROTESTANT when I first read Philippe de la Trinité's *What Is Redemption?* It was volume 25 in section 2 (The Basic Truths) of the massive 150-volume *Twentieth-Century Encyclopedia of Catholicism.* I was a Presbyterian pastor, well-schooled in the classic doctrine of the Reformation. As a Protestant I believed that God punished Jesus Christ for our sins—that in the Lord's Passion the Father saw not his divine Son, but rather our sins, and so he vented his wrath upon Jesus. Nothing would have been accomplished, said John Calvin, if Christ had only endured bodily death.

> In order to interpose between us and God's anger, and satisfy his righteous judgment, it was necessary that [Christ] should feel the weight of divine vengeance . . . [N]ot only was the body of Christ given up as the price of redemption, but . . . he bore in his soul the tortures of condemned and ruined man.[1]

In this reading of salvation, Jesus served as our *penal substitute*, receiving the retributive punishment of countless lifetimes of sin since the creation of Adam and Eve. Upon the Cross he was desolate, abandoned

---

[1] John Calvin, *Institutes* 2.16.10.

by the Father, suffering the fullness of the damnation that humankind had earned for itself.

I knew that this reading ran contrary to Catholic claims. But I knew it only because the Reformers had said so. I had not yet read a Catholic account of redemption. Would that it were so simple.

The *Catechism of the Council of Trent* declares that salvation by means of the Cross is "beyond all doubt . . . the most difficult of all" the sacred mysteries: "only with great difficulty can we grasp the fact that our salvation depends on the cross, and on Him who for us was nailed thereon."[2]

I do not think I could have chosen a better, clearer, more concise exposition than I found in this book. Nor could I have seen more stunningly the difference between classic Protestant and Catholic understandings of redemption. This book does *not* make it easy to understand the mystery. But it comes close. And the fact that it makes understanding possible—for ordinary lay readers—is something like a miracle.

As Father Philippe explains:

> Although we can and must believe that divine justice is revealed on the cross in the crucified flesh of Christ . . . it is also urgent to state clearly that the Word in his sacred flesh could only be the victim of his own merciful love.

And then this: "The stronger a man's love, the greater his capacity to suffer." And finally: "Love alone enables the Christian to penetrate the mystery of the Redeemer."

---

[2] *The Roman Catechism* I.4.5.

In these pages I learned what Catholics really believe about redemption—and I began to raise questions about the doctrine of Luther and Calvin.

Would a just God execute an innocent man for another man's crimes? Clearly the answer is no. In no system of criminal law—ancient or modern—is this possible. Yet the Reformers would have us believe that the just God would not only condemn a willing, innocent victim, but his only beloved Son! The Protestant notion of *penal substitution* (Luther and Calvin) is a close counterfeit of the earlier Catholic doctrine of *vicarious satisfaction* (Anselm and Aquinas). Both are vicarious actions, taken up by one person on behalf of others. Yet they are essentially different actions. In the latter case, Jesus willingly repays a debt he doesn't owe (ours), precisely because we owe a debt that we cannot pay, out of love. In the former case, Jesus passively suffers divine wrath and retribution at the hands of his Father.

Could an omniscient God will himself to be blind to his own Son's goodness and purity? Again, no. That would be a contradiction bordering on blasphemy. God is all-seeing, all-knowing, and all-powerful, incapable of temporary blindness or amnesia or madness. Of course the Father saw the Son as the latter hung upon the Cross. Never was the humanity of Christ so beautiful as when he hung on the Cross in loving submission to the divine will.

And if Christ served as our substitute—and endured God's wrath and suffered our punishment—then why should we still have to suffer and die? Father Philippe demonstrates that Christ was not merely our substitute. He was our representative. Thus he did not exempt us from suffering but rather endowed our suffering with divine power. He enabled us to imitate him, uniting our own sufferings to his—and even sharing in his act of redemption. Thus St. Paul could say: "Now I rejoice in my sufferings for your sake, and in my flesh I complete what is lacking in Christ's afflictions for the sake of his body, that is, the church" (Colossians 1:24). The Apostle knew that redemption was not merely personal. It was corporate. Christ willed that the redeemed should ever afterward share in the work of redemption. The rest of the story plays out in the lives of the saints.

St. Thomas Aquinas put the matter powerfully near the end of his great *Summa*. Because Christ suffered and died, "man knows thereby how much God loves him, and is thereby stirred to love Him in return, *and herein lies the perfection of human salvation*."[3]

The Passion of Christ is not a story about divine wrath and punishment. Christ's sufferings, in fact, are not punishments. They are a pure offering of love. The eternal Father did not step out of character to pummel his beloved Son. Rather, as Aquinas put it, the Father inspired the Son "with the will to suffer for us."[4] Christ suffered not the fate of the damned but the self-giving love of the divine. His Passion was an image in time of his love for the Father in eternity. He suffered out of unmeasured charity and obedience. Here is Thomas again:

---

[3] St. Thomas Aquinas, *Summa Theologiae* III.46.3, emphasis added.
[4] Aquinas, *Summa Theologiae* III.47.3.

Christ gave more to God than was required
to compensate for the offense of the whole
human race. First of all, because of the exceed-
ing charity from which He suffered; secondly,
on account of the dignity of His life which
He laid down in atonement, for it was the
life of one who was God and man; thirdly, on
account of the extent of the Passion, and the
greatness of the grief endured. . . . And therefore Christ's Passion was not only a sufficient
but a superabundant atonement for the sins of
the human race.[5]

Jesus suffered out of obedience to the Father—and a
love that extended to every human being, including his
persecutors!

For Catholics, then, redemption is not just a
decree, not a legal fiction, not a layer of snow to pret-
tify a dunghill. It is a work of divine love that makes
us a new creation in Jesus Christ. The same love that
moves the spheres empowers us to become saints. The
logic that inheres in love satisfies justice, and it also
inspires imitation and participation.

That is the doctrine of redemption, and it is the
doctrine that first converted the pagan world to Jesus
Christ.

Redemption is the message of the Gospel—the
substance of the *evangel*—and until we recover it in
its fullness, we cannot succeed in our efforts for a
new evangelization. In these pages is the best possible beginning for that task. (They even identify and

---

[5] Aquinas, *Summa Theologiae* III.48.2.

address the eight difficult Scripture passages that the Reformers cited in opposition to Catholic doctrine.) And to think that this book was almost lost! The *Twentieth-Century Encyclopedia of Catholicism* was a heroic undertaking, and it was renowned in its brief moment. The individual volumes appeared in French in the 1950s and were immediately translated into English. But there were one hundred fifty of them, and the individual contributions, many of which were superb, got buried in the grand sweep of the series.

The series itself, moreover, was soon disregarded as outdated. The Second Vatican Council took place shortly after the *Encyclopedia*'s publication, and conciliar doctrine profoundly affected almost every topic covered in the set. The publisher could hardly afford to bring out a new edition so soon after initial publication.

So Father Philippe's little book vanished for a generation, appearing only briefly in a reprint edition. Its purpose was fulfilled, in many respects, by later works, such as Cardinal Christoph Schönborn's *God Sent His Son: A Contemporary Christology*, and Michael Patrick Barber's *Salvation: What Every Catholic Should Know.*

But I have retained my deep affection for *What Is Redemption?* It is the simplest, briefest, most elegant statement I have encountered. It had, moreover, a profound personal effect on me. It led me to begin thinking as a Catholic—years before I found the courage to follow those thoughts into full communion. I could not be more pleased to see a book in print if I had written it myself.

To write these words in its praise is a duty I take up with gratitude and joy.

Scott Hahn

INTRODUCTION

The contemplative should prefer the Passion of Christ
to all else as the theme of his words

—St. Thomas Aquinas[1]

"No one," as Bergson says, "is bound to write a book,"[2] and, because no other theologian has penetrated the mystery with such serene profundity, the author of this little work on the redemption has no other desire here than to be the echo of his master, St. Thomas Aquinas.

St. Thomas, writes Chesterton, was equal to divine tasks because he was an optimist and believed in life; he might aptly have been called "St. Thomas of the Creator."[3] Certainly, and that is why he wrote so well about the Redeemer. For is not the redemption another creation, as it were, of God's love, even more beauti-

---

[1] *Commentarium in Cant. Cant.*, alt. exp., 4, 635. Quotations from St. Thomas' commentaries on the New Testament follow the recent Dominican critical edition, published by Marietti, Turin. The Vives edition is used for those on the Old Testament. References have been given for texts referred to or commented upon briefly as well as for those quoted directly.

[2] Henri Bergson, *La Pensee et le Mouvant* (France: Flammarion, 2014), 113.

[3] G.K. Chesterton, *St. Thomas Aquinas* (New York: Sheed & Ward, Inc., 1933), 13–14.

ful than the first? "I have come so that they may have life, and have it more abundantly" (John 10:10). "My Father's name has been glorified, if you yield abundant fruit, and prove yourselves my disciples" (John 15:8).

In Florence one goes to admire Fra Angelico's "Crucifixion": on the right, St. Francis of Assisi contemplates the open side of our Savior; on the left, pen in hand and ready to write, St. Thomas Aquinas contemplates his face. This parallel between the Doctor of the University of Paris and the Poverello of Assisi, the stigmatic of Alvernia, is suggestive. Chesterton writes of these two saints: "A contrast in almost every feature, they were really doing the same thing. One was doing it in the world of the mind and the other in the world of the worldly . . . their tendency, humanistic and naturalistic in a hundred ways, was truly the development of the supreme doctrine, which was also the dogma of all dogmas."[4]

But, unfortunately, how numerous are the Catholic writers and speakers who have lost sight of that compassionate love which places the mystery of the Cross in its true perspective! Instead of portraying the Savior's face in its true light and authentic dimension, they have distorted it. As a result, they have done harm to many who remain frightened at the spectacle of Christ crucified because they have failed to discover in him on their own the secret of a confidence which is diametrically opposed to anxiety and aggressiveness. The Redeemer has to be shown to such souls in his true light, that in which he was understood by St. Thomas, the Common Doctor, imbued with Scripture and the Fathers.

---

[4] *Ibid.*, 130–2, 141.

It is not our purpose to offer an abstract of a treatise on the redemption, in which most of the questions would be approached catechetically, but, rather, to present a collection of reflections and quotations, converging on Christ, "the victim of merciful love." These five words, borrowed from St. Teresa of the Child Jesus, sum up excellently the subject we wish to consider here in the spirit of St. Thomas.

In chapter I are introduced the errors we envisage: the Father did not exercise punitive justice on his Son. He was not, therefore, angry with him, and the Son himself had no sense of his own damnation. The main body of the question is then treated as follows: a synthetic view of the mystery from original sin to the triumph of the Ascension (chapter II); a fully explicit consideration in terms of theological analysis of the shedding of blood (chapters III–V). Fundamentally, the redemption of Christ appears as a superabundant vicarious satisfaction for all the sins of the human race.[5] It has nothing to do with retributive justice but gives expression to a love (chapter III) which includes and qualifies a real, but wholly merciful, justice (chapter IV). The redemption appears, furthermore, and no less essentially, as a meritorious oblation, a purchasing and a sacrifice (chapter V). This forms our framework for a theology of the shedding of blood.

A conclusion emphasizes briefly that what the mystery of Christ demands above all is love at the heart of the Mystical Body. "It is not possible to know

---

[5] Christ did not make satisfaction for his own but for our sins, and hence the term, "vicarious satisfaction," used by theology (from the Latin, *vicarius,* lieutenant, or he who takes the place of another).

how much Christ has loved us";[6] but, as St. John of the Cross writes, "put in love and you will find love."[7] And so we have to cooperate in our salvation and that of our brethren "[in] the love of God and the patience of Christ."

"The principal element in the teaching of the Christian faith is our salvation accomplished by the cross of Christ."[8] Love alone enables the Christian to penetrate the mystery of his Redeemer. The words of St. John apply here with all their force: "How can the man who has no love have any knowledge of God, since God is love?" One should not be surprised to see certain scriptural passages quoted frequently by St. Thomas. The heart alone understands the words of love, and for him they are always new. "Seek by reading, and you will find by meditating; knock by prayer, and you will be admitted by contemplation."[9] The mystery of Christ on the cross calls ultimately for the humble silence of loving adoration.[10]

---

[6] Aquinas, *Comm. in Eph.* 3, lect. 5, n. 180.

[7] Letter 22, in *The Complete Works of Saint John of the Cross*, III, trans. E. A. Peers (London: Burns, Oates & Washbourne, 1935), 296.

[8] Aquinas, *Comm. in 1 Cor.* 1, lect. 3, n. 45.

[9] *Quaerite legendo et invenietis meditando; pulsate orando et aperietur vobis contemplando,* Guigo II, Migne, *Patrologia Latina,* vol. 184, col. 476 (hereafter quoted as *P.L.* followed by volume and column number).

[10] We wish to offer here our profound thanks to all those who, in different ways, have collaborated in the present work: first and above all to the Carmel of the "Tre Madonne" in Rome, then to Fr. Baudoin de la Trinite and two of our students, Frs. Jean de la Croix and Raymond de Jésus-Marie.

CHAPTER I

DISTORTING MIRRORS

Christ's Passion was a promotion, an exaltation, not an oppression. —St. Thomas Aquinas[1]

THE DOCTRINAL DISTORTION of the mystery of the redemption which we desire to correct is characterized by one radical error: Christ, it is said, suffered on the cross in order to satisfy retributive justice. Two corollaries flow from this: one is the anger of God the Father with his Son, the other, that the Son suffered torments akin to those of the damned. But this is false. For it would be unjust and criminal to punish an innocent man instead of those who are guilty, and Jesus was not only innocent but innocence itself, and never bore the anger of God the Father nor any kind of damnation.

We shall quote at length texts which distort the features of the Redeemer in this way and, unfortunately, without the slightest difficulty, could have produced still more of them. Bossuet, Bourdaloue and

---

[1] *Comm. in Joan.* 13, lect. 1, n. 1734.

5

Massillon head the list, and are imitated, as best they can, by Gay, d'Hulst, Monsabré and still others. The libraries of religious communities, parishes, seminaries and study circles are all furnished with works giving this teaching. The labors of Rivière and Richard have undoubtedly had good results, but they have not been enough to dissipate the error; far from it.[2]

Since error may always be found in writings which are otherwise beyond reproach, it would be doing the authors we have mentioned a serious injustice to judge them solely on the texts of theirs which we shall allege here. But error is error, even when allowed to slip into the company of the purest truths, and even more dangerous then than when accompanied by other errors. Although the passages we have chosen are not all equally reprehensible, they are nonetheless disquieting inasmuch as they all give the impression that Christ was, during his Passion, the object of the Father's vengeance. This seems to us to distort the perspective of revelation on an essential point.

Nothing is so striking as contrast to show the sterling character of St. Thomas' statements concerning even the subtlest aspects of the redemption. On the one hand we find convulsions and pessimism, on the other, serenity and calm optimism. Try to adopt the aggressive mentality for a moment: an enraged God wreaks vengeance on his Son for quantities of sins of which he is innocent, finally driving him to the feeling of his own abandonment and quasi-damnation. After

---

[2] It is a pleasure to welcome Villepelet's new edition of L. Richard's *Le Dogme de la Rédemption* (Bloud et Gay, 1932) under the title *Le Mystère de la Rédemption*, in "Bibliothèque de Théologie," Series I, vol. I, (Desclée: Tournai, 1959).

that, one can better appreciate the directly opposed statements of the Angelic Doctor, calming, lucid and measured, under the banner of merciful love. Even when enduring the mortal sorrow of the Garden of Olives the Savior never experienced interiorly the least abandonment by his Father, even on the level of his human sensibility. Christ never suffered at his Father's hands. St. John did not write: God is justice, God is vengeance, but, "God is love" (1 John 4:8).

Are we, therefore, excluding justice from the work of redemption? On the contrary, justice, as we shall maintain against the deviations of liberal theology, is implied by redemption, but, just as there is justice and justice, commutative justice and distributive justice, so it is well to beware of confusion.

Commutative justice is the justice of exchange, of giving and receiving *(do ut des)*. Strictly speaking, it never enters into God's relations with creatures, nor into the creature's relations with God, and this because God, who is infinitely transcendent, is the source of everything: "What powers hast thou that did not come to thee by gift?" (1 Cor 4:7). In St. Augustine's fine and vigorous phrase, adopted by the Council of Trent, God, in crowning the merits of his saints, crowns his own gifts.[3] Sin is certainly something of our own, but as a disorder, a privation, a non-being, which offends God in his providence over us without affecting him as he is in himself. Sin had harsh repercussions on the body and soul of the Word made flesh but it makes no difference to the divine perfection.

---

[3] Council of Trent, Sess. VI, cap. 16, in Denzinger, *Enchiridion Symbolorum*, 810 (hereafter quoted as Denz.). See Ia, qu. 21, art. 1 and art. 3.

WHAT IS REDEMPTION?

Distributive justice shares out benefits and penalties in due proportion. The just ruler will govern accordingly, treating his subjects as their merits or demerits require, awarding the highest offices to the most capable, and not allowing himself to be swayed by personal considerations. Distributive justice shines out analogically in God's works, and knows no higher rule than the wisdom of infinite love, which is answerable to no one.

Retributive justice implies a judgment of the just punishment and is derived originally from distributive justice. It is exercised on the guilty alone, never on the innocent, and should, therefore, be excluded from the relations of the Father with the Son, even in the course of the Passion.[4] But does divine justice shine out in the dying, scourged and crucified Jesus? Undoubtedly, and very really, but in a different way, as, following St. Thomas, we shall explain later. Jesus does not suffer and die for his own sins but for those of the human race. He is a propitiatory victim for our sins, it is true, but in virtue of merciful love and not of retributive justice.

---

[4] We do not wish to deny God's retributive justice where sinners are concerned nor that Christ more than abundantly satisfied the requirements of this justice; but it is essential to grasp firmly that Christ could not make total satisfaction by satisfying this kind of justice alone (*ex justitia vindicativa*): for he could not be its object, he could not be punished instead of us as though substituted for us. The Catholic authors we criticize know and state that the redemption is a work of love and mercy; only it is unfortunate that they have not seen, or have not explained, clearly enough that the justice in question there could only concern loving and not retributive justice.

PENAL SUBSTITUTION

The thesis that Christ was substituted for sinners to
incur the penalties which were owing in retributive
justice to their sins, usually called the thesis of penal
substitution, is taught by Luther in his commentary on
the Epistle to the Galatians. Christ voluntarily took all
our sins upon himself as though he himself had committed them: having become a sinner, the curse itself,
it was just that he should suffer the penalty of death to
achieve our salvation as though it were the effect of a
divine condemnation.

> He himself, certainly, is innocent because he is
> the immaculate and unspotted Lamb of God, but,
> because he bears the sins of the world, his inno-
> cence is loaded with the guilt of all these sins.
> Whatever sins you or I or all of us have committed
> and shall commit, they are as much Christ's (pro-
> pria Christi) as though he had committed them
> himself. In short, we shall perish for eternity if our
> sin does not become the very sin of Christ. This
> true knowledge of Christ, as given to us by St. Paul
> and the prophets, has been obscured by some impi-
> ous sophists.[5]
>
> Since, according to the law, every thief should
> be hanged, Christ also had to be hanged according
> to the law of Moses because he took the place of the
> sinner and the thief; and not of one only, but of all

---

[5] Martin Luther, *In Epistolam Sancti Pauli ad Galatas Commentarium*, in *Opera Lutheri*, XL, Weimar edition, 435, quoted and commented by Grech, "Theoriae ad explicandam Redemptionem apud
Protestantes in Anglia cum Doctrina Catholica Comparatae," in
Doctor Communis, II–III (Rome: 1955), 86.

sinners and of all thieves.[6]

Christ truly became the man accursed according to the law, not for his own sake, but for ours, as St. Paul says.[7]

The theme of penal substitution, so understood, is, unfortunately, to be found as a matter of course in many Catholic authors who write about the divine intentions with regard to the mystery of our redemption. It is, in such cases, a postulate beyond discussion. For example:

Chardon

Every time I reflect on the oblation made by the divine mother of Jesus in the Temple, and hear the oracles which fall from the lips of Simeon, the saintly old man, and from those of Anna, the prophetess, I feel my heart touched with pity. It seems to me that Simeon's words contain, as it were, a refusal on God's part to accept the sacrifice which Mary offers him. Mother! That head is too small for the crown of thorns which I have prepared for it. Those shoulders are not strong enough to support the heavy burden of the cross. There is not blood enough in those veins to satisfy my justice. Those hands are too small for the large nails which must pierce them. Those arms and legs would not fit the length and breadth of the cross. The whole of that body offers insufficient surface for the blows of the whip which must lacerate it. Take that child away and, when he shall have reached the size and proportions necessary

---

[6] *Ibid.*, 433.
[7] *Ibid.*, 422.

if I am to exercise my justice to the full, then will be the time to bring him and present him to me.[8]

Bossuet

The thought of his innocence is the sweetest of consolations for the just man when he is afflicted; and, among the evils which overwhelm him, in the midst of the wicked who persecute him, his conscience is his refuge. . . . Jesus, the innocent Jesus, did not enjoy this sweetness in his Passion. . . . He is not even allowed, in the midst of so much shame and torment, to think in his conscience that he is being treated unjustly. Truly, he is innocent in regard to men; but of what use is it to him to know this, since his Father, to whom he looked for consolation, himself regards him as a criminal? It is God himself who has laid on Jesus Christ alone the iniquities of all.

Lower, lower your head: you have wished to be the scapegoat, you have taken our iniquities upon yourself; you will carry the whole weight, you will pay the debt to the full, without respite, without mercy.[9]

His Father delivered him up in the interests of justice; Judas out of self-interest. . . . Jesus has taken up voluntarily the world's iniquities, the justice of his Father wished to avenge them on his person.[10]

---

[8] Louis Chardon, *La Croix de Jésus*, I, 154–5 (Paris: Lethiellieux, 1895).

[9] Jacques Bénigne Bousset, *Oeuvres oratoires de Bossuet* (Lille-Paris: de Brouwer et cie, 1891), III, 362–364.

[10] *Ibid.*, V, 205, 206.

WHAT IS REDEMPTION?

Massillon

The soul of the Savior in his agony. . . , that soul purer and holier than all the heavenly intelligences, sees itself soiled of a sudden with all our iniquities: with eyes of a divine modesty it sees itself covered with the most shameful excesses of sinners; with those eyes of clemency it beholds itself blackened by their hatreds and rages; with those eyes of the most lively religion it sees itself sullied by their impieties and blasphemies; in a word, it sees itself soiled with all their vices. . . . Ah! how gladly would our Savior turn his innocent gaze away from this frightful object; but his Father's justice compels him to attend and forces it upon him in spite of himself; it is an unrelenting light pursuing him, and it does not allow him to be spared one moment of the intimate spectacle of the total ignominy with which he is covered. He would undoubtedly have expired, such was the severity of these trials, had not the justice of his Father been keeping in reserve for him longer torments and a finer sacrifice.

Righteous Father! Was more and yet more blood still necessary in addition to this interior sacrifice of your Son? Is it not enough that it should be shed by his enemies? And must your justice hasten, as it were, to see it shed? See how far this God, whom we believe to be so good, carries his vengeance against his own Son whom he beholds carrying our sins.[11]

---

[11] Jean-Baptiste Massillon, *Oeuvres de Massillon*, I, 518, col. 2, col. 1–520, col. 2 (Paris, 1843).

Avrillon

> Jesus abandoned by his Father. This is not the least afflicting nor the least painful part of the forestalled Passion both of mind and heart which Jesus Christ endured in the Garden of Olives, before shedding his blood and dying on Calvary. Judge of the excess of his grief by what an only Son would feel who, persecuted and abused by the whole world, although innocent, and worthy of being loved by the most savage and barbarous hearts, should see himself on the point of suffering the most cruel agonies, and the most unjust and infamous death; who in this extremity should have recourse to an all-powerful Father who could deliver him, and make him triumph over his enemies; and that this Father, far from taking his part or giving him refuge, notwithstanding his prayers and tears, should abandon him, and himself should send to pronounce sentence of death.[12]

Monsabré

> God found in his Christ what he would have sought in vain in other victims: the sin to be punished. . . . In him God sees, as it were, sinfulness itself. . . . And, filled with the horror which iniquity inspires in divine holiness, Christ's sacred flesh becomes an accursed object in our stead. . . . He was mankind, the universal man, substituting for sinners of every

---

[12] Avrillon, *Conduite pour passer saintement le temps du Carême*, 93–4 (Lyons-Paris, 1840). English translation: *A Guide for Passing Lent Holily*, 79–80 (London, 1844).

place and time, at once man and mankind. At the sight of him divine justice forgets the common herd of human beings, and has eyes only for this strange and monstrous phenomenon from which it is to take satisfaction. Spare him, Lord, for he is your Son! No, he is sin: he must be punished![13]

He is the man accursed *par excellence,* the curse made man, according to the Apostle's vigorous phrase.[14]

Maucourant

Justice will wreak terrible revenge. Mankind will be given the part of least suffering; it is another—man in order to suffer, God in order to expiate sufficiently, man-God in order to mediate between God and man—who will bear all the weight of the divine vengeance. . . . He is in the Garden of Olives, in torments under the weight of our sins and of his Father's justice.[15]

Parra

Jesus knows with his divine knowledge the deep malice of sin which is the evil opposed to God and his own personal enemy, and which calls of itself for divine vengeance. He appreciates perfectly the absolute justice of the divine cause against him, he knows that he must be struck down; nor is he

[13] Jacques Marie Louis Monsabré, *Carême de 1881,* in Jean Rivière, *Le Dogme de la Rédemption,* 4th edn. (Louvain, 1931), 242.

[14] Monsabré, *Carême de 1880,* in Rivière, *ibid., 242.*

[15] Abbé Maucourant, *La vie d'intimiti avec le bon Sauveur* (Nevers, 1897), 23.

unaware of any of the measures God may apply when he wishes to take his revenge. Knowing all that, he beholds himself, the universal sinner, the sin of mankind, in the presence of a God resolved upon the utmost exaction of his revenge. There is only the truth here, only what is perfectly just; he has wanted it from the first moment, when he offered himself impetuously to make up for the insufficiency of human expiation. Here I am, O righteous God; strike me! And henceforward God does strike him.[16]

THE WRATH OF THE FATHER

Calvin, also, accepts the thesis of penal substitution. "Our absolution consists" he writes, "in this, that the obligation to be punished has been shifted to the Son of God. This compensation is to be kept in mind above all else if we are not to tremble with fear and anxiety throughout our lives, as if we were still threatened by that just vengeance of God which the Son of God took upon himself."[17] God avenged himself justly on God made man: "If Christ had died a bodily death only, this would have contributed nothing to our redemption; on the other hand, it was especially valuable that he should feel simultaneously the severity of the divine vengeance and that, in answering for us before God's justice, he should thus satisfy his righteous judgement."[18]

On such a view one must speak of the enmity or

---

[16] Charles Parra, *L'Evangile du Sacre-Coeur*, 43–4 (Toulouse, 1931).

[17] John Calvin, *Institutio christianae Religionis*, cap. 16, quoted and commented by Grech, *loc. cit.*, 88.

[18] *Ibid.*, col. 376.

wrath of the Father with his Son. Such expressions continue to signify the exercise of retributive justice on the Savior because of our sins.

Nouet

> If he looks upon his Father, Jesus is terrified by his wrath. His distress is so extreme that he kneels like a wretched criminal who awaits his death sentence and attempts to soften its harshness. He adopts the most humble of postures in order to turn away his Father's anger but, as he sees it to be inexorable and knows that he must die, his heart, already terribly alarmed and horrified at the appalling horde of evils which are paraded before him, splits, as it were, in half, the one part fleeing death in horror, the other wanting it with unconquerable resolution. One part trembles under the scourges of God's wrath, the other respects and accepts them. One part fears the torments, the other desires them. Each part pulls him in its own direction with such violence that he succumbs and suffers mortal convulsions; all of him, his very being, is one cruel martyrdom, since he makes efforts on himself such that they cause his whole nature to topple, and which would have killed him a hundred times over if God had so desired.[19]

Bossuet

It was necessary that all in this sacrifice should be

---

[19] Jacques Nouet, *Nouveau Cours de Méditations* (*selon la methode de saint Ignace*) *sur la Vie de Notre-Seigneur Jésus-Christ,* 11 (Paris), 206, 206–7.

divine: a satisfaction worthy of God was necessary, and it was necessary that a God should make it; that there should be a vengeance worthy of God, and that God himself should take it.

"The face of God on evil-doers," that is, the face of justice. God shows his Son this face, he shows him this flaming eye; he beholds him, not with that look which brings serenity, but with that terrible look "which lights fire before it" . . . with which he strikes terror into the conscience; he beholds him, then, as a sinner, and advances upon him with all the resources of his justice. My God! Why do I see against me this face with which you astound the reprobate? . . . I see only an irritated God. . . . The man, Jesus Christ, has been thrown under the multiple and redoubled blows of divine vengeance. . . . (God) rejected his Son and opened his arms to us: he looked at him in anger, and gave us a look of mercy. . . . As it vented itself, so his anger diminished; he struck his innocent Son as he wrestled with the wrath of God. This is what passed upon the cross, until the Son of God read in the eyes of his Father that he was fully appeased and saw, at last, that it was time for him to leave the world.[20]

It is an unheard-of prodigy that a God should persecute a God, that a God should abandon a God; that an abandoned God should complain, and that an abandoning God should prove inexorable: but it is to be seen on the cross. . . . Jesus suffers the disdain of a God, because he cries out, and his Father hears him not; and the wrath of a God, because he prays, and his Father answers him

---

[20] Bousset, *Oeuvres oratoires de Bossuet,* III, 379, 382, 383.

not; and the justice of a God, because he suffers, and his Father is not appeased. He is not appeased for his Son, but he is appeased for us. When an avenging God waged war upon his Son the mystery of our peace was accomplished.[21]

Massoulié

In order to understand in a few words the full implication of the Passion and what David conveys in one verse of a psalm, I picture to myself Jesus Christ on the cross, who, while undergoing his greatest sufferings, complains to his Father and says to him: You know, O eternal Father, that in the Garden of Olives I made you my prayer with all possible humility, and that I asked you to be pleased to take away this chalice from me; but, nevertheless, you have turned away from me and have rejected my plea (Ps 88:16–17).

What, finally, most afflicts me and fills me with inexpressible sorrow is that you will now look on me in anger—"I am overwhelmed with thy anger" (Ps 87:17)—and cause me to suffer the full weight of your indignation. Alas! eternal Father, what has impelled you so to abandon your own Son? "Why hast thou forsaken me" (Ps 21:12)? Nevertheless, it was necessary that the eternal Father should exercise this justice on his Son. . . . and that his sufferings and torments should end only with his life.[22]

---

21 Bousset, *Oeuvres oratoires de Bossuet,* IV, 286–7.
22 Antonin Massoulié, *Traite de L'amour de Dieu* (Brussels, 1866), 489–91.

Wiseman

It is not a fear of being immolated, as the lamb to take away sin, that oppresses his heart; but a dread of being sent forth as the scapegoat with the frightful crimes of all the world upon his head. But this is not all. As the bearer of this load, he necessarily becomes an object of the wrath of his own eternal and dear beloved Father! He, the dutiful, the most loving of sons, who had but one will with the Father, who throughout his mortal life, had been the perfect pattern of all obedience and docility, he who actually, at that moment, was going to suffer that he might give the first example of an obedience even unto death, is under the wrath, to say no more, of that tenderest of Fathers! Oh, what abundant cause of fear! Who can wonder that he dreaded so dark a state, and recoiled before such a charge![23]

Faber

But is there cruelty in God? No! Infinite justice is as far removed from cruelty as infinite love can be. Yet it was the Father, he who represents all kindness, all indulgence, all forbearance, all gentleness, all patience, all fatherliness in heaven and earth, who chose that moment of intensest torture, when the storm of created agonies was beginning to pelt less pitilessly because it was now wellnigh exhausted, to crucify afresh, with a most appalling interior crucifixion, the Son of his own endless complacency. . . . Mary gave up the Son to the Father. She sacrificed

---

[23] Nicholas Wiseman, *Meditations on the Sacred Passion* (London, 1909), 47–8.

the love of the mother to the duty of the daughter. . . . She heard the outcry of his freshly crucified soul, pierced to the quick by this new invention of his Father's justice. And she did not wish it otherwise. She would have him abandoned, if it was the Father's will. And it was his will. Therefore. . . .[24]

Gay

Fervently emulous of her holy Son, Mary offers herself with him, like him, and in him, with an inexpressible appreciation of the rights of God, of his decrees, and of his ways, of his justice and what it demands, of his wrath and what interprets it, of his avenging acts and what they accomplish. . . . She abandons herself without the least reserve into the hostile and incensed hands of the divine creditor, who requires inexorably the last penny from his debtor, and whom only the most drastic shedding of blood can satisfy.

Jesus becomes the real and voluntary substitute for all human iniquity, the conscious receptacle of all human filth, the sewer of the whole of creation. . . . It is in this guise and in all the reality of this condition of sinfulness that he presents himself to his Father, to the justice, the holiness, and, necessarily, to the wrath, the rebukes and the curses of his Father: and this as one in every way

---

[24] Frederick William Faber, *The Foot of the Cross, or The Sorrows of Mary,* 308–9 (London, 1859). The author continues: "No one would have dreamed that a human soul could have held so much love as she poured out upon Jesus at that moment . . . [her heart] rushed into his soul as if it would fill up with its own self the immense void which the dereliction of the Father had opened there."

like us and clothed in all our weaknesses as really as in our crimes.

I assure you that, though it be true that Jesus could not and did not for one moment cease to be in himself the object of the Father's good pleasure and of God's infinite love, nevertheless, inasmuch as he had taken our crimes upon himself and had made of himself the place, receptacle and treasury of our iniquities; inasmuch as he represented universal evil, he had not the shadow of a right to the shadow of a mercy, and I do not think it would be rash to say that that merciful shade did not refresh him for one instant during the consuming hour of his Passion. The Passion of Jesus revealed nothing but wickedness and excess on the part of men and devils. On the part of God it revealed only what was just, just with an unmitigated and absolutely rigorous justice. . . . Behold, then, this sacred, blessed, all pure and all holy soul, which held evil in, as it were, infinite abhorrence and loved God as all the Seraphim together will never love him, as Mary will never love him; behold it, then, before this God aroused, locked in combat with this irritated and hostile God who is armed for battle and wages war.[25]

Josefa Menendez

(Christ says:) I offered myself to achieve the work of redeeming the world. At that moment I saw upon me all the torments of the Passion, the calumnies,

---

[25] Charles Gay, *Conferences aux Mères Chrétiennes,* II (Paris, 1877), 228, 514, 515, 523–4. Other passages of this type may be found in Boüessé, O.P., *Théologie et sacerdoce* (Chambery, 1938), 83–4 , all of which are rightly condemned by the author.

the insults. . . . All these pains forced themselves on my sight, together with the hordes of offences, sins and crimes which would be committed down the ages. . . . Not only did I see them but I was clothed in them . . . , and, under this burden of disgrace, I had to present myself before my most holy Father and implore his mercy. Then I felt breaking over me the wrath of an offended and irritated God, and I offered myself as a scapegoat, I, his Son, to calm his rage and appease his justice.[26]

Longhaye

Yes, yes, do not let us fear for Jesus' dignity, do not let us enervate the Gospel. Jesus is afraid. And for whom and of what? First of all, for himself and of his approaching Passion. . . . But of what is he afraid besides this? Of the justice and the wrath of God. He appreciates them as no one else; he feels their whole weight upon him, and they cause him to tremble in all his being. . . .

What does he suffer, Jesus, the universal penitent as he is the universal sinner? What contrition is his! . . . I have my own explanation of his terror. It is for my sake, in my place, that, as a voluntary victim, he falls, throws himself into the hands of the living God. Consistently with his role and with himself, he wishes to experience to the depths of his soul how horrible that is. . . . He thinks it right and just to feel the terror of the divine wrath which he has diverted to himself.[27]

---

[26] Josefa Menendez, *Un appel d l'amour, Le message du Coeur de Jésus au monde et sa messagere Soeur Josefa Menendez* (Toulouse, 1944), 402.

[27] G. Longhaye, *Retraite annuelle de huit jours d'apres les exercices de*

THE TORMENTS OF HELL?

Calvin, in the course of expounding the article of the creed, "Christ descended into hell," examines the two most widely spread explanations of his time: either Christ was buried or he descended into limbo to proclaim the redemption to the souls of the patriarchs. He rejects the first as tautological and the second as fabulous, and gives the following explanation of his own. If Christ had undergone a corporeal death only, then our bodies alone would have been redeemed, which is impossible; if, then, our souls have been redeemed, Christ must be said to have suffered the punishments which threatened them because of sin, that is, the punishment of eternal death. "He descended into hell" means for Calvin that Christ bore the sorrows of eternal death for us.[28] "Thus it was necessary that Christ should wrestle hand to hand, as it were, with the hordes of hell and with the horror of everlasting death. . . . If, then, he is said to have descended into hell, there is nothing surprising in his having suffered the death which an enraged God inflicts upon criminals."[29]

This talk of the torments of hell in connection with Christ the Redeemer may also be found to a greater or lesser extent among Catholic authors and writers. Some affirm a kind of pain of damnation, despair included.

Bourdaloue

It was in view of this that the eternal Father took a course of action as adorable as it was rigorous and,

---

saint Ignace (Paris-Tournai), 435, 438.

[28] Grech, *loc. cit.*, 88–9.

[29] Calvin, *Institutio christianae Religionis*, edit, cit., col. 376.

forgetting that he was his Son and regarding him as his enemy (forgive me these expressions), declared himself his persecutor or, rather, the chief of his persecutors.

Strike, Lord, strike now: he is ready to receive your blows; and, without considering that he is your Christ, see him only to remember that he is ours, that is, that he is our victim and that, in immolating him, you will satisfy that divine hatred you have for sin. God is not satisfied with striking; he seems to wish to reprobate him by leaving and abandoning him in the midst of his torture: *Deus meus, Deus meus, ut quid dereliquisti me?* This abandonment by God is, in a way, the pain of damnation, which, as St. Paul says, Jesus Christ had necessarily to undergo for us all. The reprobation experienced by men would not have sufficed to punish sin to the full extent of its malice: what was necessary, if I may be permitted to use such language (but you will penetrate its meaning, and I have no fear that you will understand it in Calvin's sense), was that the sensible reprobation of the God-man should fill up the measure of the curse and of the punishment due to sin. Not at the last judgement will our irritated and offended God satisfy himself as God; nor is it in hell that he declares himself authentically to be the God of vengeance; Calvary is the place he has chosen: *Deus ultionum Dominus.* On Calvary his vindicative justice is free to act without restraint, untrammelled, as it is elsewhere, by the smallness of the subject who is made to feel it: *Deus ultionum libere egit.* All that the damned will suffer is but a half-revenge for him; all that gnashing of

teeth, those groans and tears, those inextinguish-
able fires, all that is nothing, or almost nothing,
compared with the sacrifice of the dying Jesus
Christ.[30]

Grou

The abandonment of Christ by his Father may
be said to have commenced in the Garden of
Olives. From the moment of his entrance there,
he appeared in the eye of God as a criminal laden
with all the iniquities of the human race. How
appalling that weight of crime, and how deserving
of the most terrible maledictions, and most terrific
punishment! The desolation consequent on that
abandonment continued to increase throughout his
Passion. . . . We cannot reflect without a shudder
on the nature of that awful dereliction. It was not
real assuredly, for never was Jesus Christ so justly
the cherished object of his Father's complacency as
in the hour when he gave him the strongest manifestation of his devoted love; but, although merely
apparent, and exerting no influence over the inner
depths of the soul, it produced an impression ago-
nizing beyond the reach of created intelligence to
conceive. It was in a manner equal to the pain of
reprobation, or that caused by the loss of God, a
torment which is exclusively the portion of the
spirit, and incomparably the most intolerable of the
sufferings of hell. . . . Hence we may form a conception of the desolation of the soul of Jesus Christ.
That desolation was accompanied, it is true, with

---

[30] Louis Bourdaloue, *Op. cit.* x, 157, 159–61.

imperturbable peace, because it had no admission to the interior sanctuary of his spirit, nevertheless, it was inconceivably bitter, receiving no alleviation from the prospect of future comfort, which Jesus Christ voluntarily excluded from his views.

To understand the desolation of Jesus Christ, we must measure it by another standard, that of the punishment due to the sins of past, present and future generations, for which he satisfied the divine justice not only strictly but superabundantly. Of the frenzy and despair which are exclusively the portion of the reprobate, he could have no experimental knowledge but, with the exception of these sensations, he felt the bitterness attendant on the loss of God more acutely than all the demons and damned put together.[31]

Gratry

It seems to the Son of God that God also is against him. He, who comes to unite men among themselves and with God, in order to bring back even the most abandoned of them, undergoes the trial of absolute separation from men and God. And so it is that the Son of man truly bore for us the *pain of hell!*[32]

Fouard

Never has one who was dying felt the abandonment

---

[31] Jean-Nicolas Graou, *L'Intirieur de Jésus et de Marie*, II (Paris, 1838), 79–81. English translation: *The Interior of Jesus and Mary*, II (Dublin, 1847), 72–3.

[32] Alphonse Gratry, *Commentairs sur l'Évangile selon Saint Matthieu* (Paris, 1909), 313

of God as Jesus did, since no one but he has lived by
and in God. Jesus, become sin for our sakes, made
a "curse" and an "execration," as St. Paul says, suffered something so terrible at God's hands that no
human words suffice to describe it. In that hour,
heaven veiled itself and hell alone remained before
the Savior, who glimpsed an eternal despair as
infinite as the God whom it avenges.[33]

A Trappist Monk of Sept-Fonts

At that moment he was the world's greatest criminal; never was there such a one before: the sinner of
sinners, the sinner representing all sinners.

What shame, what agonies, what heartbreak, it
was for you, O my Jesus, when you presented yourself, laden with our iniquities, before your Father,
that most holy God, most beloved Father, most
severe Judge! . . . Abandoned by his Father he suffers a kind of hell.[34]

Le Camus

Jesus had insensibly bowed his head to the ground
under the crushing burden which he was making
his own. But suddenly the infuriated countenance
of God, of which he just catches a glimpse, shatters
his soul. He can bear it no longer and, rising, cries:
"Father, if it be possible, and with you all things are
possible, let this chalice pass from me!" This, then,

---

[33] Constant Henri Fouard, *La vie de Notre-Seigneur Jésus-Christ*, II
(Paris, 1905), 387, 388.
[34] *Soixante-quinze Méditations sur la Passion de Notre-Seigneur Jésus-
Christ* (Torurnai, 1925), 8, 9, 109.

has nothing to do with Satan. It is with his Father alone that Jesus wishes to drive the hideous bargain. Will divine justice deduct nothing from the overflowing chalice? Is sin, then, so great an injury that it must be expiated by so frightful a reparation? Death he accepts; but his Father's curse, will he be able to bear it? And yet he must, since, Lamb of God, though innocent of sin, he is taking the place of sinners. It is because he took their place that his beseeching cry did not penetrate heaven and that the name of the Father, pronounced with such love, remained ineffectual on his lips. It is said that the Savior then suffered all the torments of hell save despair.[35]

Parra

He must expiate for our sins in our place; he must, then, clothe himself in them as in an infected garment which has been dragged in the mud; he must shoulder them and take the whole responsibility for them before his Father as though he had committed them himself. . . . He pants, he is ashamed and, finally, he allows a sob of disgust to escape him; he cannot bear the sight of himself any longer, he cannot bear himself. *Coepit taedere*; are we to say that he disgusts himself? Disgusted with himself, he also feels disgust taking hold of him for his mission and the task of redeemer for which

---

[35] Le Camus, *Op. cit.*, 389. The author continues: "What is certain is that the emotion of his soul shattered his whole physical being." But it is simply untrue to say that our Savior suffered all the pains of hell, even if we except despair.

he has offered himself. . . .

He is the condemned divinity and, although he cannot be damned since he is God, he feels the frightful terror of the damned whom the divine hand hunts down, tortures and overwhelms. If hell could harbour among the damned one who would not hate God, and who would believe in a final pardon, Jesus in Gethsemani would be he, subject, abandoned, like the iron in the fire of the forge, to the hatred of God so ardently bent on punishing in him the sin he personified. Bowed down with his face to the ground and without daring to raise his eyes, he groans, trembles, bleeds in all his body, and craves pity from his judge—who remains deaf to him.[36]

A contribution from Fr. Perroy is worth including in order to round off and crown our evidence lest it appear too scanty.

He (Jesus) was born to ascend Golgotha, and to ascend it as a victim; for was he not first and above all, the Victim of Expiation? He knew this, he felt it in every fiber of his being, he had willed it, and his heavenly Father so regarded him. The foremost reason for Christ's earthly existence, his chief role, was to satisfy the justice of God, to repair the outrage offered to God, to cherish God's honour. It would seem, almost, as though the salvation of mankind came second. To satisfy God's perfect justice, Jesus must pay the full debt, and receive no mercy. For more than four thousand years this supreme expiation was being prepared . . . the divine wrath had

---

[36] Parra, *L'Evangile du Sacre-Coeur*, 30–2, 35, 44.

accumulated from century to century against sinful humanity. Now and then through the ages God's finger moved, sketching, in rough, broad strokes an outline of his anger, to be filled in, in the course of time. [Here the author recalls the red heifer immolated opposite the Temple, the scapegoat chased across the valley of Cedron, Isaac, Job, Jonas.]

Now at last the time is accomplished: the real victim promised through the ages, has come. Christ is born, and it is with jealous care that God guards him until he ascends Calvary to pour forth his blood. There is, first, the remote preparation, a slow gathering, as it were, of an outraged justice. [Having recalled the crib, the exile, persecution and obscurity, the toil and exhausting work of the apostolate, Fr. Perroy continues:] All, all are instruments of vengeance in the hands of God. . . . [37]

Had Christ been only human, to be rejected by all men, and abandoned by his own; to have heaven, his sole hope closed against him, would have cast him into an abyss of despair. . . . "My God, my God, why hast thou forsaken me?" . . . God hearkened not to the call of his Son; nay, more, he rejected him. His hand, far from reaching out to rescue Jesus from the angry flood, plunged him deeper into its turmoil. Oh, God, thou hast become so cruel to thine only Son! But this is the hour of eternal justice. . . . What appalling dereliction! Yet Christ must suffer it.

"I could have evaded this cruel payment for sinners," says Jesus the God. "The choice was left

---

[37] Louis Perroy, *La Montée du Calvaire* (Paris), 7–8, 10. English translation:
The Ascent of Calvary (New York, 1922), 6–8.

to me; and I willed to cast myself into this fathom-
less sea, from whose depths I can rise no more. . .
. From the just anger of God I cannot flee; I must
suffer all, and unto the end." All this Christ could
have said to himself, and added that bitterest sting
of despair: "Not only am I bereft of all human help,
but I am judged unworthy of divine succor." . . .

I have abandoned God—and Jesus, bearing
on his body all my cowardly betrayals, suffered the
frightful chastisement due me for all eternity. The
dereliction: terrible retaliation: an eye for an eye, a
tooth for a tooth.

But this death is my salvation; and because of
the abandonment in which this divine Sinner ago-
nizes, covered with my sins, I shall be blessed and
pardoned, and shall never taste the bitterness which
he has drunk. His last satisfaction of divine justice
was the supreme act of generosity. Love could go no
further to expiate our sins and reassure our souls.[38]

REACTIONS

Rivière and Richard, who rank as authorities in questions concerning the redemption, state categorically
that the passages we have just quoted do not echo the
authentic teaching of the Church.

Rivière

However much allowance we may feel disposed
to make in these passages for rhetorical exagger-

---

[38] *Ibid.*, 315–21. The latest edition of this work (1958) brings its sales
to the seventy-five thousand mark. The lapse we have indicated is
all the more to be regretted since Fr. Perroy's book otherwise well
deserves its success.

ation, we are bound to admit that they rest on a completely false idea. This sanguinary, cruel God is not the God of reason, still less is it the God of the Gospel. Catholic doctrine cannot be made responsible for such statements as those to which we have just listened.[39]

Richard

No doubt this oratorical theology was intended to bring home all the horror Christ feels for sin, an unquestionable truth upon which we ought to meditate. But such exploitation of the scriptural and traditional concept of Christ's atonement distorts the true meaning of the Gospel. . . . The Pauline texts which are brought forward do not really mean to say that Christ experienced the effects of God's "wrath" for all who commit sin. That would be, as Pierre Corneille said in the eighteenth century appealing to the commentaries of the Fathers, "an insufferable blasphemy unknown in past ages. Christ could not think that God was angry with him. He knew that he loved God, his Father, and that he was very dear to the Father. . . ."

The kind of abandonment in which Jesus would experience God's wrath in his soul is utterly foreign to patristic tradition as also to that of the great thirteenth-century doctors. "The best theologians of the sixteenth century, whether Dominicans with Cajetan, or Jesuits with St. Robert Bellarmine and Suarez, hold faithfully to the teaching of the great thirteenth-cen-

---

[39] Jean Rivière, *Le Dogme de la Rédemption*, 241 (Paris, 1931).

tury doctors and reject this novel account of the dereliction whenever they encounter it."[40]

The words of Fr. Bouèssé are also much to the point: "The gentle and tenderly human sublimity of the divine pardon is distorted by the shocking errors which so many books and sermons contain."[41]

And Fr. Dehau writes:

> We in France, in our turn, have often allowed Jansenism to falsify our minds and, especially, our imaginations. It inspires too many works, not sufficiently distrusted, which give us a picture of the mystery of the redemption with the divine justice raging over its victim. But, on the contrary, it is love. . . . To attribute what belongs to divine love to divine justice is a perversion worthy of the devil. Possibly those who do this are unaware of the fact; the evil is no less grave. It would be a maneuver typical of the devil: to deprive love of its adorable victim and make him the victim of justice.[42]

This is the truth and we must admit it frankly. Fr. Mersch writes: "Christ answering before God for the world's sins appears as the total sinner, the damned among the damned, crushed under the most complete and utter divine wrath. But the truth is very different; for Jesus' work is diametrically opposed to hell. Hell is hatred, opposition to God, oneself and humanity; Christ's work tends to love and union."[43]

---

[40] *Ibid.*

[41] *Op. cit.,* 83.

[42] Pierre-Thomas Dehau, *Le Contemplatif et la Croix,* Éditions de l'Abeille, I (Lyon: 1942), 76–8.

[43] Emile Mersch, *La Théologie du Corps Mystique,* 2nd edit., I (Paris), 345.

"Ultimately," writes Fr. Pro, "all this retributive justice, this bargaining, this notion of a ferocious God seem to us to verge on blasphemy."[44]

St. Francis de Sales would certainly have agreed with such judgments. This much is indicated by his words about a "certain small treatise, lacking the names of its author, of its printer and of the place of its publication."

> If the author means by "sufferings" the merit and value of our Lord's sufferings he is right to say that they are infinite; but then he expresses himself badly in describing them as sufferings, sorrows, miseries, the cup of God's ire and abandonment by God: he had better have described them as so much consolation and sweet saving water which quenches for ever the thirst of those who drink it. . . .
>
> This same author is again inaccurate if he means that the sufferings themselves are infinite because to drink of God's anger and to be abandoned by him are infinite evils: but such does seem to be his meaning when he says that the Savior drank the cup of God's wrath and when he places the descent into hell among the events of the Passion. This last he would relate, no doubt, to the fear which Calvin attributes to Jesus Christ when he says that he feared for the salvation of his own soul and was afraid of the malediction and anger of God. But, as I have already shown, this is an insufferable blasphemy since fear presupposes a probability that what one fears will come to pass, and hence assumes that our Lord felt the probability of his own damnation—a

---

[44] Pro, "Vivre de Dieu," in *La Vie Spirituelle,* May 1959, no. 450, 498.

truly horrifying assumption.[45]

Right as it is to criticize the thesis of the divine wrath venting itself on its innocent victim, it is no less necessary to replace it with another account of the mystery, for, as Auguste Comte says, one only destroys what one replaces.[46]

---

[45] St. Francis de Sales, *Oeuvres Completes,* III, "L'Estendart de la Ste Croix," in *Sermons* (Paris, 1833), 154, 213, 214–15.

[46] Masure writes that "what M. Rivière has had to criticize above all is a certain type of Gallican eloquence which we all know well and which rests on an excessively narrow juridical foundation; it explains Fr. Sanson's objection on behalf of the agonized souls which it thus puts into chains." "Le Redempteur," in *Le Christ, encyclopedie populaire des connaissances Christologiques* (Paris, 1932), 537. This is true, but Fr. Sanson has also failed to maintain a balanced position since he goes to the opposite extreme of liberal theology. See Fr. Sanson's *Le Christianisme, mitaphysique de la charite,* Ve Conference (Spes, 1927), 23. Fr. Sanson rightly takes to task the thesis according to which Christ redeemed us "by taking our places in order to undergo the just consequences of divine punishment. . . . A strange justice, indeed, which seeks compensation from the innocent for the misdeeds of the guilty. . . . The distance is great indeed between the God who is so offended by his creature that he can only take upon himself the vengeance his justice demands, and the God of goodness by whom our existence is explained! This theory depends on an analogy with barbarian law and customs. Those who formulated it under the influence of their age and circumstances usually corrected its 'simplisme' and harshness by finding in Christ the essential goodness they failed to find in God. But it would be disastrous to cling to it or to return to it" (pp. 6–7). The truth is that this author only seems to know one theory of reparation, that which he criticizes (pp. 6–7). What does the redemption hold for him that is positive? Only this, and it is radically incomplete and insufficient: "Christ is the missionary, the universal and perpetual spokesman of divine goodness, to stimulate us to this task (that of becoming good), direct us, support us in the task, help us to take it up again when we collapse," etc. (p. 10). "Christ not only furnishes us with a lesson in generosity, his role is deeper and more essential than that," "he creates in us the obli-

WHAT IS REDEMPTION?

Nevertheless, the Charybdis of punitive justice is not to be avoided at the price of falling into the Scylla of a denial of all justice, which dogma in any case does not allow. What is wanted is a balanced approach to the subject. St. Thomas is, as we shall now see, the teacher *par excellence* of this balanced approach.

---

gation to be generous" (p. 20). "Christ is not substituted for us to provide a ransom, to repair an injury, or to pay a debt, no matter to whom; that would only be an external salvation. He does infinitely more for he obliges us to the life of charity which is the divine life itself," etc. (p. 21).

But, as we shall see, there is far from being any opposition between satisfaction and divine charity.

CHAPTER II

THE PLAN OF THE REDEMPTIVE INCARNATION

The economy of the Christian religion is ordered
principally to the Resurrection of Christ.
—St. Thomas Aquinas[1]

Original Sin

THE SCANDAL OF THE CROSS follows on the scandal of
original sin. This last dogma is not to be minimized on
the erroneous pretext that redemption must be understood in terms of our personal sins. There is no room
for private judgment. One has either to accept revelation or to leave it, however disconcerting it may seem
at first sight. It is curious that now, when humanity
is becoming increasingly aware of its dimension as a
community, it should still reject the dogmas of a sin
and a redemption on such a universal scale.

As against racists we claim with reason the same

---

[1] *Comm. in Tim. 2*, lect. 2, n. 49.

fundamental rights and duties for every man coming into this world. St. Thomas Aquinas and Pascal are in agreement here: "Just as the various members of the body form the parts of a human person so all men form parts and members of human nature."[2] "Men of all generations should be considered as the same man."[3] There is neither Jew nor Greek, freedman nor slave, all are one. Nor is there anything arbitrary about the fact that God has twice over, on different but complementary planes, recapitulated all humanity, as it were, in a single pair: first, in Adam and Eve, our first parents; then in Jesus and Mary, the new Adam and the new Eve. Humanity, once marvelously endowed with gratuitous riches in the state of original justice, has been still more marvelously redeemed from its sin under the sign of the cross.

Man passes his own comprehension. He is not only a problem to himself but a mystery as well. Considered under either of the twin points of view of justice and mercy, divine government infallibly respects what is personal and characteristic in every member of humanity. At the same time it is equally true that the destiny of each in particular is included in that of the community, not only on the various sociological levels (of family, profession, nation), but also on the supernatural level: all are sinners in Adam, all are redeemed by our Savior. We do not live in isolation.

The dogma of mankind's fall in Adam and Eve does nothing to injure the rights of human nature as these can and should be conceived by right reason. Original sin deprives us of the supernatural gift of sanctifying

---

[2] *Comm. in Rom.* 5, lect. 3, n. 410.

[3] Blaise Pascal, *Fragment d'un traité du vide* (1647), preface.

grace and of the preternatural gifts, to none of which could we lay any rightful claim—and of nothing else.[4] In the same way original sin is in us from birth as what is called a sin of nature, that is, one which lacks the connotation of personal responsibility and personal punishment, even to the extent found in venial sin.[5]

No more than the angels can man lay claim to the possession of God in the vision face to face: "That end which consists in the vision of God and is eternal life is above the nature of every creature."[6] That is why the souls of infants who die unbaptized are in limbo and "there possess without pain that which belongs to them by nature."[7] "They suffer no interior distress and enjoy their happiness in peace."[8] The fact that they have not received Baptism "will not cause them sorrow, any more than the fact that they have not received many graces granted to others like them causes sadness in the wise."[9]

Our human nature knows the interior struggle between flesh and spirit (Gal 5:17), and that this nature may suffer and die. Those who deny original sin are as aware of it as we are. But, from the point of view of philosophical reason alone, these facts do not entitle us

---

[4] "Nor is there anything contrary to the order of justice in this, as though God were punishing the sons of Adam for the sin Adam himself had committed. For this punishment is simply the withdrawal of gifts which God had given to the first man and which were to be handed on to others through him; hence these gifts were only due to others in so far as they were designed to be handed on by heredity" (*Compendium Theologiae*, cap. 195, n. 372).

[5] *De Malo*, qu. 5, art. 1, ad 9um.

[6] Ia, qu. 23, art. 1 corp. Cf. *De Malo*, qu. 5, art. 1, ad 15um.

[7] *Ibid.*, art. 3 corp.

[8] *Ibid.*

[9] *III Sent.*, qu. 71, app. 1, art. 2.

to infer with certainty a real communal fall of human nature. In other words, although it is of faith that our first parents enjoyed the privilege of immortality, and that their lower appetite only became concupiscence, in the pejorative sense, after the first sin and as a penalty, there is nothing we can learn in the light of reason alone which would oblige us to admit as much; we should be left with a mere motive in favor of the credibility of revelation.

It is important that here we should follow the great Thomist theologians such as Cardinal Cajetan and the Carmelites of Salamanca. In answering the questions, Is our human nature wounded? Is it fallen? these authors make a fundamental distinction: if we mean historically fallen, in relation to its first condition of original justice in Adam and Eve, the answer is, Yes: if we mean philosophically fallen in its intrinsic constituent elements, then the answer is No. From this point of view human nature is neither fallen nor vitiated nor wounded. God could, in the beginning, have created the human race in its actual state of weakness, ignorance, suffering and mortality without there having been any fall from a state of perfection, the fugitive reality of which in the dawn of humanity is a fact guaranteed for us by revelation alone.[10]

> Original sin is the lack of original justice according to which man's reason was harmoniously ("secundum aequitatem") subservient to God, and the lower faculties to reason, and the body to the soul:

---

[10] See our article, "Dieu de Colere ou Dieu d'Amour," in *Etudes Carmelitaines, Amour et Violence* (1946), 93–105, Original Sin. The question still remains partially under discussion among theologians.

but this harmony ("aequitas") is disrupted by original sin since, once reason has ceased to be subject to God, the lower faculties rebel against reason, and the body is withdrawn from obedience to the soul by corruption and death.[11]

This is an historical and not a philosophical fall: "The Church does not admit that man is nothing but corruption and sin in the sight of God. On the contrary, original sin does not appear to her to have affected his aptitudes and powers fundamentally but has even left essentially intact the natural light of his intellect and his liberty."[12]

St. Thomas gives us a golden rule we must observe if we are to steer a straight course in interpreting the state of original justice: "What we believe," he says, "we

---

[11] *Comm. in Rom.* 4, lect. 1, n. 335.

[12] Pius XII, Discourse of September 25th, 1949, to the International Congress of Humanistic Studies. Does this mean, without any further qualification, that if humanity had been created in a state of pure nature it would not, in the last analysis, be any better or worse than it now is *existentially*? From this point of view we answer unhesitatingly that, apart from Christ and his historical and sacramental influence on the one hand, humanity would not be as good as it now is at its best; and that, apart from the devil and his perversity on the other, it would not be as evil as it now is at its worst. That is to say, humanity would be altogether more mediocre. At the same time, we cannot question the presence of the evil one, at whose door *also* we must lay the failures in justice and charity, the perpetual avarice and hypocrisy, which continue down the ages and were so severely stigmatized by our Lord. Also, we know from the Vatican Council that "the Church is of herself, because of her excelling sanctity and inexhaustible fruitfulness in all that is good, because of her Catholic unity and unconquerable stability, a great and perpetual motive of credibility, and an irrefragable witness to her divine mission" (Sess. III, cap. 3. Denz. 1794). As in goodness, so in evil, man is beyond the grasp of man. The present state of humanity is not "natural."

owe to authority; it is by faith that we hold whatever is beyond our grasp naturally speaking. In the same way, when something is not guaranteed by divine authority, we should respect the nature of things."[13] We may be allowed to think, however, that St. Thomas was not being sufficiently true to himself when he credited Adam, the patriarch of humanity, with universal infused knowledge.[14] This seems both exorbitant and implausible in, to take but one example, the realm of mathematics. The medieval doctors had a "grandiose notion" of the state of innocence which requires "serious modification."[15]

Nevertheless, St. Thomas was not indulging in mythology in his interpretation of Adam's immortality: the latter was not, according to him, "intrinsically protected *(ab intrinseco)* against every external mortal danger, such as a sword-stroke and so forth, but divine providence took care of him,"[16] This is perfectly reasonable. In the same way we would say that snakes have always crawled and lions have always been fierce and carnivorous. There is no good reason to doubt the fact of original justice, just as there is none for unduly prolonging its supposed duration.

But the most important point is that our first parents recapitulated the whole of humanity, and their (in certain respects) quasi-angelic state made clear that God's plan was to treat the whole human race

---

[13] Ia, qu. 99, art. 1. Cf. Ia, qu. 68, art. 3 corp.

[14] Ia, qu. 94, art. 3.

[15] These phrases are taken from Fr. Labourdette's *Le peche originel et les origines de l'homme* (Paris, 1953), 65, which may be consulted with profit. See especially: "L'Etat d'Innocence et la Chute," 65–90, and "La Perfection de l'Etat Originel," 169-82.

[16] *De Veritate*, qu. 24, art. 9 corp.

as a single immense family and to regale it with life and happiness beyond all that it had a right to expect. The point of departure had been given. The choice for or against God would be made in the most favorable circumstances, with a perfect knowledge of what was involved and in the name of humanity.

But man is no more able than the angels to claim his independence in relation to God, the ultimate moral end. Nor, once his duty of loving submission to God has been acknowledged, can he lay claim to any privilege of impeccability. Even supposing Adam had not sinned we should still have been tested and have had to choose for or against God. This is inseparable from the nature of every created spirit. St. Thomas repeats it often; thus, "The power to sin is not, in itself, essential to free will, but is a consequence of liberty in a created nature."[17] "There does not and could not exist any creature whose free will was so confirmed in goodness that it would belong to it as of natural right not to be able to sin."[18] "Considered in that which they are by nature, both men and angels can freely turn to evil."[19]

Adam and Eve were happy and enjoyed a perfect equilibrium beyond the simple condition of human nature, and yet they sinned. There was no excuse, no extenuating circumstances for this sin. At the devil's instigation they revolted against God in a movement of pride which had their full consent.[20] Sanctity demands fundamentally that each should lovingly accept his

---

[17] *Ibid.*, art. 7, ad 4um.

[18] *Ibid.*, corp.

[19] *Ibid.*, art. 3 corp. See our three articles on the peccability of angels in the natural order, in *Ephemerides Carmeliticae*, I (1957), 44–92, and II (1958), 338–90.

[20] IIa IIae, qu. 163.

creaturely condition just as he finds it. So, also, in the case of Adam and Eve; only they said, No. In whatever way they sinned (the matter of the sin, the fruit, is disputable and may be thought of simply as a symbol), their sin was grave, in the same way as that of the rebellious angel.[21]

They saw themselves as naked, stripped of their privileges, in the clutches of the prince of this world, the liar and murderer, and they were ashamed. The devil, as symbolized by the serpent, was really the instigator of the sin of our first parents. The human drama continues the angelic drama. This is an important point if we are to safeguard the balance of the revealed truths which throw light on our condition in the world. It is well emphasized by Fr. Bouyer:

> For the Fathers, fallen human nature was not merely a nature deprived of God's gratuitous gifts and reverting to its proper condition, but it was a human nature made captive by the devil. In their eyes the fall did not consist primarily in a process of detachment from God and attachment to self, but in attachment to the devil rather than to God. Thus they could retain, without contradiction, the idea of a nature which was fundamentally good and so forth, but fallen in such a way that it could not rise again by its own strength. Indeed, man, in detaching himself from God, was far from becoming his own master; he became, on the contrary, the slave of the devil.[22]

---

[21] Ia, qu. 63, art 2.

[22] Louis Bouyer, "Les deux Economies du Gouvernement Divin: Satan et le Christ" in *Initiation Theologique*, II, 531. English translation— not used here—*The Theology Library*, II (Chicago, 1955), 492. "It

We should here recall the teaching of our Lord himself:

> If you are Abraham's true children, it is for you to follow Abraham's example; as it is, you are designing to kill me, who tell you the truth as I have heard it from God; this was not Abraham's way. No, it is your father's example you follow. . . . You belong to your father, that is, the devil, and are eager to gratify the appetites which are your father's. He, from the first, was a murderer; and as for truth, he has never taken his stand upon that; there is no truth in him. When he utters falsehood he is only uttering what is natural to him; he is all false, and it was he who gave falsehood its birth (John 8:39–44; cf. Matt 12:37–39).

We neither can nor should abstract from the devil in the history of the fall and redemption. The prince of this world, who thrice, but without success, tempted Christ at the beginning of his public life, made his entry into history in the times which followed the creation of the first man and woman; and he, the evil one, the liar, the murderer, remains in our history day in, day out, calling evil good and good evil, freely confusing truth and falsehood together. All too often the

---

would seem that all modern accounts suffer from a hidden contradiction" because they have failed to give his place to the devil. One is then confronted by "this alternative: either consider human nature as radically evil in itself from its first creation, which is Manicheism" because "fallen man is then, properly speaking, man fallen to his rightful level and reduced to his own natural resources. . . or else neutralize the consequences of the fall, which is Pelagianism. But for the Fathers the question appeared quite differently because there was a third term: the devil" (*ibid.*).

devil has the knack of managing to make people think he does not exist. On the contrary, he both exists and acts. The life of the Curé d'Ars is, in its way, an eloquent witness to the fact. The outline of the evil one is to be discerned in the shadow of many a politician, philosopher or man of letters, and in that of all whose profession is vice. Such things as Masonic initiation ceremonies and nocturnal black masses—horrible, valid and sacrilegious—are a sad reality. But although the devil is not to be ignored, we should not try to see him everywhere; we should only remember that "[he] goes about roaring like a lion, to find his prey" (1 Peter 5:8). This is an article of our faith.

From an essentialist and abstract point of view the physical death which is natural to man is a perfect *symbol* of sin, for, once separated from God, its life, the soul is no better than a kind of spiritual corpse. From an historical and existential point of view, however, and in the light of revelation, much more can be said: for death is, *also*, the fruit of the sin instigated by the devil, which thus made its entry into the world of mankind (Rom 5:12, 21; 6:23).

It is one thing to philosophize on a basis of legend, quite another to perceive the deep spiritual meaning in an historical datum. The unbeliever might say that it has all happened *as though* death had entered the world because of sin, meaning by this that no fitter parable than that in Genesis could be found to teach the desired doctrine of the malice of sin. We should reply that it is not a matter of a parable here but of a moral and dogmatic teaching inscribed in historical facts. God may "write" by directing events as well as by inspiring his sacred authors, though without violating his creature's liberty and without allowing himself to become its slave. This is one of the manifestations of his omnipotence. The action of Adam and Eve expresses a whole series of philosophic, dogmatic and moral truths, and was itself the prelude to another action, that of the redemption, the culminating point of revelation. All that occurred between Genesis and the Gospel was a figure (1 Cor 10:2).[23]

In a deep sense, then, and one which acknowledges the presence here of the supernatural and the miraculous, we say that the mystery of original sin, as it is described in Genesis and proposed authentically by the Church's magisterium, is essentially pedagogical, but pedagogical in so sublime a fashion that it can inscribe theology in history.

THE INCARNATION AND THE CROSS

The human race, prone now to sin, suffers, weeps, bleeds and dies. But it was not ennobled simply to be disinherited. Instead of asking ourselves what might have happened if Adam and Eve had not sinned let us confine ourselves to a wise and prudent meditation on the data of revelation. The dogma of original sin is, in fact, linked to that of the redemption in an historical continuity from which it may not be abstracted. To the tree of the knowledge of good and evil there corresponds the tree of the cross; to the proud disobedience of our first parents, the lowly obedience of the Son of God made man, "the first born among many brethren" (Rom 8:29). All are sinners in Adam, all are

---

[23] See the remarkable article of Fr. de Lubac, "A propos de l'allegorie chrétienne," in *Recherches de Science Religieuses,* I (1959), 5–43.

redeemed by the Savior: "Everything is for you. . ., and you for Christ, and Christ for God" (1 Cor 3:23). In fact God would not have permitted the great family of mankind to be lost in Adam and Eve through the devil's instigation, unless he had meant it to be saved again in Jesus and Mary, the new Adam and new Eve. Shadow implies and only makes sense in terms of light, so that we can only appraise it in terms of light. "It would not have been necessary for Christ to die for all if all had not died through Adam's sin; but just as all did die in Adam, so all are brought to life in Christ" (1 Cor 15:22).[24]

There has not been and never will be anything natural about our destiny. The fate of a mankind vainly raising its towers of Babel will always scandalize and dishearten those who deny the fact.

From the first days in Genesis God had given more than he owed it to himself to give. He will give still more. *Mirabiliter mirabilius*: he has marvelously fashioned the dignity of human nature and he wishes to refashion it still more marvelously.

This is the mystery of the redemptive Incarnation, which, in some way, deifies the entire human race. In relation to God, in relation to man, and from the only point of view which matters ultimately—that of love and its manifestation to the praise of the glory of God—the redemption is more astounding than the creation, for all the beauty of the latter. God is love, and love is the secret of all his permissions and decrees. A harmonious continuity with love is the basis for our optimism.

But what is the ultimate meaning of this for us?

---

[24] *Comm. in 2 Cor.* 5, lect. 3, n. 184.

That the sign of the cross leads us to love better and more truly than did happiness. For God only permits the evil of our sufferings and sins so that they may make way for still greater gifts such as, on the one hand, humility in the accepted certitude of our personal inability to do good, in the denial of our evil will, and in detachment from what passes and is not God; and on the other, a confident faith in God's merciful love and in the blossoming of the three theological virtues which are the pledges of all the divine riches. These are the two poles, negative and positive respectively, of the sanctity of the Gospel. It is a simple matter ultimately.

It is the *Noverim me, noverim te* (knowing myself I should know thee) of St. Augustine, and his *Ama et fac quod vis*, when properly understood. It is the *Todo-Nada* of St. John of the Cross: the *all* of God, the *nothing* of what is not God. "We have an everlasting city, but not here" (Heb 13:14). It is the little way of St. Thérèse of Lisieux: that one lose one's soul to find it, like a child of God.[25] It is the way of all the saints: "All is grace for those who love God" (Rom 8:28, my translation).

And, finally, the sorrow in the hearts of all of good will is to be turned into joy in the possession of God. This light and momentary affliction brings with it reward multiplied every way, loading us with everlasting glory; if only we will fix our eyes on what is unseen, not on what we can see. What we can see lasts but for a moment; what is unseen is eternal (2 Cor 4:17–18). But, in order to penetrate the depths of this great mys-

---

[25] In the prayer at Mass on Easter night the Church makes us ask God to preserve in us "the spirit of adoption." This "spirit of adoption" is the spirit of spiritual childhood, the paschal grace *par excellence* of recovered innocence.

tery, we must fix our eyes before all else on the divine person of our Redeemer.

Just as man, when he wishes to reveal himself, expresses the thoughts of his heart with a word, and, as it were, clothes them in letters or sounds, so God, when he wishes to reveal himself to men, clothes with flesh in time the Word which he has conceived from all eternity. No one comes to have knowledge of the Father save through the Son who has said: "I am the door; a man will find salvation if he makes his way in through me" (John 10:9).[26]

A secret of love

The redemptive Incarnation is the expression of divine love which, in order to appear the more tender and the more deep, chose the way of mercy and pardon. "God has abandoned all men to their rebellion, only to include them all in his pardon" (Rom 11:32). It is *de facto* as our Redeemer that God has given us the beloved Son whom he concealed in his Father's heart.

St. Thomas is insistent in his affirmation of the primacy of charity in the mystery of the incarnate Word. All the riches of the Incarnation and redemption are, he writes, the work of charity *(totum est opus charitatis).* It was for love that he became man, for love that he died. All his mysteries spring from the immense love of God which is beyond the knowledge of any creature. We simply cannot conceive it *(incomprehensibilis cogitatu).*[27]

"No question of it, it is a great mystery we worship. Revelation made in human nature, justification won

---

[26] *Comm. in Joan.* 14, lect. 2, n. 1874.
[27] *Comm. in Ephes.* 3, lect. 5, n. 178.

in the realm of the Spirit; a vision seen by angels, a mystery preached to the gentiles; Christ in this world, accepted by faith, Christ on high, taken up into glory" (1 Tim 3:16). Faced with this triumphal song of St. Paul, St. Thomas' only recourse is to multiply short excerpts from Scripture:

> A mystery (*sacramentum*, Vulgate) is something sacred and secret. But there is nothing as secret as that which we have in our hearts, and this is even more true of that which is both sacred and secret in the heart of God. "No one else can know God's thoughts but the Spirit of God" (1 Cor 2:13). "My secret to myself" (Isa 24:16, Douay). "Thou art a hidden God" (Isa 45:15, Douay). And this is the Word of God in the heart of the Father *(et hoc est Verbum Dei in corde Patris)*. "Joyful the thoughts that well up from my heart" (Ps 45:2). This secret is a sacrament of mercy whereas the secrets of men are sometimes vain: "The Lord looks into men's hearts and finds there illusion" (Ps 93:11).
>
> This mystery is one of mercy inasmuch as it is for the restoration of the world. It is great because it is the true God himself, great beyond limit. This secret, therefore, which is hidden in the heart of the Father has become man. . . . Just as the Word hidden in the heart is made manifest in a sensible word so the Word of God, hidden in the heart of the Father, became manifest in the flesh: "The Word was made flesh and came to dwell among us" (John 1:14).[28]

---

[28] *Comm. in Tim.* 3, lect. 3, n. 130–1.

God appeared as man

The person of the Son of God is not a human person, nor is the divine nature a human nature (otherwise we should have a contradiction in terms); but the Son of God, while remaining God in his divine person and nature and the Word begotten by the Father from all eternity, made his own a human nature in assuming a soul and body like ours. The Son of God thought, willed, loved and acted like a man in every respect in which this was not incompatible with his dignity as Son of God and purity itself.

Four comparisons may be enlisted to help our reflection on this great mystery, but only the fourth has any positive value. They correspond to the four ways of envisaging possession or assimilation.

1. The thing possessed transforms without itself suffering alteration *(mutat et non mutatour)* So, for example, when wisdom is acquired by a dunce the latter becomes wise but wisdom does not become stupid.[29]

2. The thing assimilated effects a change and receives a change *(mutat et mutatur)*. So food in relation to the man who has eaten it.[30]

3. The thing assumed neither changes him who assumes it nor suffers change in itself *(non mutat nec mutatur)*. For example, when a ring is slipped on to the finger.[31]

---

[29] But the assumption of the humanity changes nothing in God. God as he is in himself is unchangeable, and neither the Incarnation nor the creation modify him in any way. The change is not on his side but on that of the creature (as against any kind of anthropomorphism).

[30] But the human nature remains as such unaltered in its own proper constitution (as against Monophysitism which proposed a kind of confusion of the natures).

[31] But the human nature of Christ is enriched through being assumed

THE PLAN OF THE REDEMPTIVE INCARNATION

4. The thing possessed is changed in itself without changing its possessor (*non mutat sed mutatur*). Such is the case when a garment adopts the shape of the human body and such is also the case of the human nature which was assumed by Christ. It is united to the Person of the Word in such a way that it is ennobled and filled with grace and truth: "We had sight of his glory, glory such as belongs to the Father's only-begotten Son, full of grace and truth" (John 1:14).[32]

The problem of Christ's human consciousness has been much discussed among certain theologians during the past twenty years, and often in the following terms: how could this man know that he was the Son of God? Presented in this way, the problem seems to us to become unreal, since this man *is* the Son of God in so far as he is a self-conscious subject, identical with the divine nature: he *knows* that he is the Son of God because he *is* the Son of God. Once the mystery is properly stated, the answer follows naturally. But there still remains the different and inverse question: how does the Son of God know that he is man? He knows it because he has consciously, as God, assumed a human consciousness.[33] Though there are undoubtedly two

---

(by grace, knowledge, the virtues).

[32] *Comm. in Philip.* 2, lect. 2, n. 61.

[33] Christ does not have *self*-awareness in virtue of his human consciousness. As Fr. Kleutgen put it so well when the preparatory drafts of the Vatican Council were being drawn up, one must reject as inapplicable to Christ the expression, "self-conscious nature" (*natura sui conscia*), for the person alone is self-conscious. On the level of free theological discussion one may be allowed to think that to hold the contrary position and allow some validity to the expression "human *nature* conscious of *itself*" leads logically to the Nestorian heresy in positing two subjects, and consequently two persons, in the Incarnate Word. This amounts to a denial of the mystery of

consciousnesses in Christ in virtue of his two natures, divine and human, Christ is, nevertheless, *only one single conscious subject (unus sui consciens)*. There is in him but one single person, that of the Son of God, the second Person of the Blessed Trinity, knowing himself to be at once God and man in virtue of his two consciousnesses in his two natures.[34]

In the vivid words of St. John, the Word became flesh. As he comments on this verse St. Thomas asks himself why St. John does not mention the soul, for the Word assumed in his person both the body and soul of man.

He replies that St. John wished to emphasize the truth of the assuming of flesh against those who denied the fact because they considered the flesh to be a creature of the devil, using, for example, our Lord's words to his disciples after the Resurrection: "Touch me, and look; a spirit has not flesh and bones as you see that I have" (Luke 24:39).

St. John also wished to emphasize God's goodness to us. The assuming of a human soul would already have been the sacrament and sign of a great love, but how much more so this stooping of the Word to our very flesh! "No question of it, it is a great mystery we worship. Revelation made in human nature" (1 Tim 3:16).

St. John wished to throw into relief the exceptional

---

the hypostatic union. See the author's "A propos de la conscience du Christ, un faux probleme theologique," in *Ephemerides Carmeliticae,* 1960, I.

[34] One does not have to investigate, therefore, how this man can know that he is the Son of God, but one must simply believe this mystery: the Son of God consciously became man and this man *is* God; it is God who says "I" in this man.

character of the union realized in Christ. Where other men are concerned, God unites himself to their soul only; in the case of our Savior alone does the Word of God unite himself to our flesh.

Finally, St. John wished to intimate that the Incarnation befitted the work of redemption. Since man was wounded in his flesh, he would be healed by the flesh of the Word. "This was something the law could not do, because flesh and blood could not lend it the power; and this God has done, by sending us his own Son, in the fashion of our guilty nature to make amends for our guilt. He has signed the death warrant of sin in our nature" (Rom 8:3).[35]

God made man is the Redeemer

In becoming man, the Son of God could be at once the priest and victim of his sacrifice, and so give evidence of the greatest possible love, for "this is the greatest love a man can show, that he should lay down his life for his friends" (John 15:13).

This he did. He could not have given more.

> Because it was necessary that Christ should have something to offer, he offered himself. This offering was pure, since his soul lacked any stain of sin: "It must be a male yearling lamb, or a male yearling kid, that you choose, with no blemish on it" (Exod 12:15). It was also fitting, since it is fitting that a man should satisfy for men: "He offered himself as a victim unblemished in God's sight" (Heb 9:14). It was also suitable for immolation, since his flesh was mortal: "God sent his Son in the fashion of our

---

[35] *Comm. in Joan.* 1, lect. 7, n. 169.

guilty nature" (Rom 8:3). Again, it is identical with him to whom it is offered: "My Father and I are one" (John 10:30). It also unites those for whom it is offered with God: "That they may all be one; that they, too, may be one in us, as thou, Father, art in me, and I in thee" (John 17:21).

But, it will be objected, Christ's flesh belongs to this world. Our reply is that only materially speaking does it belong to this world: "The whole world is given over to the power of wrong-doers" (Job 9:24). For there are reasons, also, why it does not belong on earth. First, because of the hypostatic union: "He who comes from above is above all men's reach" (John 3:31), because, that is, of the Son of God who assumed this nature to himself. Because, also, of its origin, since it was fashioned by the Holy Spirit. And, finally, because of the fruit it was to bear; for the immolation of this flesh was to obtain an eternal and not a temporal benefit: "You belong to earth, I to heaven; you to this world, I to another" (John 8:23).[36]

The work of our redemption is marvelous because it is the doing of a God and a man. "As man, Christ became our sacrifice and redeemed us with his blood . . . as God, it is through him that our sins are forgiven and we are rid of the guilt of sin."[37]

No other satisfaction would have been so fitting. Man could not make satisfaction because the whole human race was in the hold of sin. The angelic nature could do no more since a satisfaction leading to the

---

[36] See *Comm. in Hebr.* 8, lect. 1, n. 384 and n. 386.
[37] *Comm. in Col.* 1, lect. 3, n. 28.

glory of the beatific vision is beyond its power. The perfect satisfaction would have to come from one who was both a God and a man, and be made for all mankind. Christ, because he died as God made man *(per mortem Dei et hominis)* destroyed the devil's power over death.[38]

The human race, having been lost by a man, has been redeemed by a man, and it was a kind of justice that man should so redeem mankind; but the man in question was God, and herein lies the infinite mercy, failing which this justice would not have been possible.

> When he says that Christ makes atonement for our sins (Heb 1:3), the Apostle shows—and this serves to emphasize Christ's dignity—the courageous activity *(strenuitas)* and marvelous diligence *(industria)* which our redemption involved.
>
> His diligence is to be seen in that he merited, through his Passion in the nature he had assumed, that which belonged to him already in his nature as God: "He accepted an obedience which brought him to death . . . that is why God has raised him to such a height" (Phil 2:8). For to forgive sins belonged to him in the divine nature, but now it belongs to him also by the merit of his Passion.[39]

The Son of God is the Redeemer

God is three Persons, the Father, the Son and the Holy Spirit. The Father and the Holy Spirit could also have become man, but in fact it is the Son who was made flesh, and it is he who offered himself for our redemption.

St. Thomas will now bring home to us that, if Christ

---

[38] See *Comm. in Hebr.* 2, lect. 4, n. 143.
[39] *Ibid.*, 1, lect. 2, n. 37. See *Comm. in Ephes.* 1, lect. 2, n. 18–19.

redeemed us as *God*, there is also a special appropriateness that he should have done so as the *Son of God*, the perfect image of the Father, Wisdom and Law *par excellence*, the first-born heir among a multitude of brethren. The mercy of the first-born Son was called for by our wretchedness as prodigal sons. These considerations help us to grasp better the spirit of adoption and spiritual childhood which should characterize our relations with God thanks to his mercy and pardon.

It is fitting that Christ should purify us of our sins both because he is God and because he is the Son of God.

As God. Because sin has its seat in the will which God alone can incline towards the good. "There is no riddle like the twists of the heart; who shall master them? Who but I, the Lord, that can see into man's heart, and read his inmost thoughts . . . ?" (Jer 17:9–10). "It was ever I, ever I, that must be blotting out thy offences, for my own honor's sake" (Isa 43:25). "Who can forgive sins but God and God only?" (Luke 5:21).

As Son of God. Four points may be considered here. Every sin is an iniquity, a transgression of the *eternal law* and divine justice. "They have broken God's law, traversed the decree he made for them, violated his eternal covenant with men" (Isa 24:5). But the eternal law and the divine justice proceed from the divine Word; hence it was fitting that Christ should remit our sins: "He uttered the word of healing and saved them" (Ps 106:20).

The light of reason is a participation in *divine wisdom*. But all sin clouds reason, that is to say, God's wisdom in mankind. "They follow a false path, that plot mischief" (Prov 14:22). It belongs, therefore, to divine wisdom to correct the sinner. "We preach Christ, the power of God, the Wisdom of God" (1 Cor 1:23). "Ever since the world began wisdom was the salve they used, that have won thy favor" (Wis 9:19).

Sin distorts the *image of God in man*. But Christ is the image of the Father: "It remains for us, who once bore the stamp of earth, to bear the stamp of heaven" (1 Cor 15:49).

The sinner has lost his *eternal inheritance*, as a sign of which Adam was shut out of Paradise. But the Son is the heir: "If we are his children, then we are his heirs too" (Rom 8:17). "Then God sent out his Son on a mission to us. He took birth from a woman, took birth as a subject of the law, so as to ransom those who were subject to the law, and make us sons by adoption" (Gal 4:4–5).[40]

The first-born Son, Innocence itself, has redeemed all his brethren who were prodigal children of the same Father, his Father and theirs.

Christ on the cross

"The proclamation was written in Hebrew, Greek and Latin" (John 19:20). This was in order that there should be no one who could not read it and because these three languages were pre-eminent among the rest: Hebrew, because of the worship of the one God; Greek, because of the wisdom of the Greeks; Latin, because of the power of the Romans. Thus these three nations laid claim to their dignity on Christ's cross, as St. Augustine says. And this especially in that Hebrew signified the conversion of devout and religious men; Greek, that of

---

[40] *Ibid.*, 1, lect. 2, n. 38–9.

the wise; Latin, that of the powerful. Or, again, in that by Hebrew it was signified that Christ would triumph over theological wisdom, for the knowledge of divine things was given to the Jews; and by Greek, over philosophical wisdom and natural science, for the Greeks cultivated these by the sweat of their brow; and by Latin, that Christ was to triumph over moral philosophy, for it was in this field that the Romans excelled. In short, the meaning was that every mind should be made to surrender to Christ's service, as St. Paul writes to the Corinthians (2 Cor 10:5).[41]

"The rock was Christ" (1 Cor 10:4), and the clefts in the rock are the wounds Christ received for our salvation: the piercing with nails, the blow from the spear. The dove, that is, the Church, loves to tarry in these clefts, because she has placed all her hope of salvation in the Passion of her Savior.[42]

Victory over sin and the devil

"Our faith, that is the triumphant principle which triumphs over the world" (1 John 5:4). The Redeemer has freed us from sin, the punishment due to sin, and the power of the prince of this world in so far as we place our confident trust in his infinite mercy. As St. Paul writes: "It is in him and through his blood that we enjoy redemption, the forgiveness of our sins—so rich is God's grace" (Eph 1:7).

---

[41] *Comm. in Joan.* 19, lect. 4, n. 2422.
[42] *Comm. in Cant.* Cant. 2, 567.

Sin is opposed to justice as death is to life, but God has restored to us his grace in Jesus Christ. We have been forgiven the punishment due to our sins: "What was the ransom that freed you from the vain observances of ancestral tradition? You know well enough that it was not paid in earthly currency, silver or gold; it was paid in the precious blood of Christ; no lamb was ever so pure, so spotless a victim" (1 Pet 1:18–19).

Above all, Christ's death on the cross has released us from the slavery itself of sin: "Look, this is the Lamb of God; look, this is him who takes away the sin of the world" (John 1:29). "It was fitting that Christ should suffer, and should rise again from the dead on the third day; and that repentance and remission of sins should be preached in his name to all nations" (Luke 24:47).[43]

St. Thomas writes at length of the victory Christ gained over the rebellious angel: the Savior came so that "by his death he would depose the prince of death, that is, the devil" (Heb 2:14).

What is meant by "depose the devil"? Not his destruction in his substantial nature, for he is incorruptible, nor, as Origen maintained, his conversion from malice, but rather the breaking of his hold over death: "Sentence is now being passed on this world: now is the time when the prince of this world is to be cast out" (John 12:31). "The dominions and powers he robbed of their prey, put them to an open shame, led them away in triumph" (Col 2:15).[44]

---

[43] *Comm. in Ephes.* 1, lect. 2, n. 18. See *Comm. in Hebr.* 1, lect. 2, n. 40.
[44] *Comm. in Hebr.* 2, lect. 4, n. 141. The context of this quotation also

"Everything helps to secure the good of those who love God" (Rom 8:28), even sin, as St. Augustine comments; not that sin can be the cause of good, far from it, since sin is evil *par excellence*, but because sin can and should be for us the occasion of more humility in a greater confidence in the merciful love of God. The devil's attacks can only strengthen the just man in the practice of the three theological virtues. "God writes straight with crooked lines."[45]

THE RESURRECTION AND ASCENSION

The Resurrection

The Passion only makes complete sense when taken together with the Resurrection; the good and the evil it involved were only (respectively) willed and permitted in view of this triumphal Resurrection, the culminating point of our Savior's life on earth.

Theologians rightly distinguish objective from subjective redemption. The former means the activity of Christ which is for our redemption, the latter, the application to each one of us of this redeeming activity through the practice of the virtues and the reception of the sacraments. The point which matters most for us here is that Christ's Resurrection belongs essentially and inseparably to redemption in the objective sense, so that, had it not taken place, this redemption would not be *what it is.*

---

repays reading.

[45] Quoted by Paul Claudel at the head of *Le Soulier de Satin.*

It is also true that the Resurrection was a glorification due to the Savior himself. "He (Christ) lowered his own dignity, accepted an obedience which brought him to death, death on a cross. That is why God has raised him to such a height, given him that name which is greater than any other name, so that every thing in heaven and on earth and under the earth must bend the knee before the name of Jesus" (Phil 2:8–10).

But this is not all—or, rather, it is all provided that we understand it correctly. For Jesus is the head of the Mystical Body, and the glorification of the head is not only inconceivable without that of the members but postulates, entails and *realizes* this.

In other words, our redemption is not an abstract notion, however rich and complex, but a living person, the Person of the Son of God made man. Jesus, though not a human but a divine person and the second Person of the Blessed Trinity, is, nevertheless, man and true man. Having died, he now rises again and overcomes death as head of the Mystical Body. As he is the Redeemer of all mankind, so all men accompany him in his own Resurrection. In the sight of God, for whom a thousand years are as but a day, who sees all in his everlasting present, all men have already risen again because of Christ, and if, for some, this is not a resurrection to life and everlasting happiness, the responsibility for this inefficacy does not lie with the Redeemer who shed all his blood for each and every one. The elect, who rejoice in the beatific vision, share the glory and happiness of the redeeming Word in virtue of his Passion, death and Resurrection, of his Ascension and sitting at the Father's right hand. It was all for our salvation, *propter nostram salutem,* and this salvation itself is for the praise of the glory of the Son and the Father in the unity of their Spirit.

St. Thomas, following St. Paul, strongly emphasizes this connection between the mysteries of our salvation. Christ's sacred humanity has saved us through
the cross, but *also* through his Resurrection and Ascension. His Resurrection has conquered both physical
death and the death caused in us by sin. As St. Paul
says: "It will be reckoned virtue in us, if we believe in
God as having raised our Lord Jesus Christ from the
dead: handed over to death for our sins, and raised to
life for our justification" (Rom 4:24–25). ". . . So that
just as Christ was raised up by his Father's power from
the dead, we too might live and move in a new kind of
existence" (Rom 6:4). And St. Thomas says:

> It was from his divinity that all the sufferings and
> actions of Christ had their power to save us, because,
> as St. John Damascene says, Christ's humanity was
> in some way the instrument of his divinity. But
> effects resemble their causes: to Christ's death,
> therefore, which was in him the extinction of mor-
> tal life, there corresponds the extinction of sinful
> living in us, while the justification by which we
> return to the new life of justice *(novitatem justitiae)*
> is said to have been caused by the Resurrection by
> which he returned to a new life of glory.[46]

Christ became our justice, our peace, in short, our
redemption, in a positive way by his Resurrection, and
St. Thomas gladly insists on this, for him, fundamental
point of view.

---

[46] *Comm. in Rom.* 4, lect. 3, n. 380.

Christ's Resurrection is the first and general cause of all resurrection properly speaking, and so it must be the cause of our resurrection; as the Apostle writes to the Corinthians: "Christ has risen from the dead, the first fruits of all those who have fallen asleep; a man had brought us death, and a man should bring us resurrection from the dead" (1 Cor 15:20). And this is only reasonable since God's Word is the life-giving principle of all mankind. . . . The Word of God gave life first of all to the body which he assumed; now, by means of it, he causes the resurrection of all other bodies.[47]

But the resurrection of bodies is but secondary compared with the resurrection of souls which have died through sin.

Because its power is drawn from his divinity, Christ's Resurrection works for the resurrection of souls as well as of bodies. For it is due to God both that the soul live by grace and that the body live by the soul. It follows that Christ's Resurrection has effective power by which it may be instrumental in the resurrection of souls and bodies. Similarly, Christ's Resurrection is the exemplar of the resurrection of souls; for our souls must be conformed to the risen Christ. "So that," as the Apostle says, "just as Christ was raised up by his Father's power from the dead, we too might live and move in a new kind of existence. We have to be closely fitted into the pattern of his Resurrection, as we have been into the pattern of his death . . . and you, too, must think of yourselves as dead to sin, and alive with a

---

[47] IIIa, qu. 56, art. 1 corp.

65

life that looks towards God, through Christ Jesus, our Lord" (Rom 6:4, 11).[48]

St. Thomas' thought can be seen precisely and synthetically expressed in the following text:

> There are two elements in the justification of a soul, namely, *remission* of sin, and *renewal* of life by grace. If we speak of justification as it is effectively caused then we are speaking of the divine power and must say that both the Passion and the Resurrection are its causes (in so far as both are instruments). But if we speak in terms of exemplary causality then we connect the remission of sin—by which we become dead to sin—with Christ's Passion and death, and say that his Resurrection is the cause of our new life through grace or justice. As the Apostle says: "He was handed over to death for our sins," that is, in order to take them away, "and raised to life for our justification" (Rom 4:25). But Christ's death is also a cause in virtue of his merits.[49]

St. Thomas does not shrink from writing with emphasis: "There are many mysteries of Christ upon which we should meditate, but upon none so much as the Resurrection; round this revolves the whole economy of the Christian religion *(totus christianae religionis status):* "Thou canst find salvation if thou wilt use thy lips to confess that Jesus is the Lord, and thy heart to believe that God has raised

---

[48] *Ibid.,* art. 2, corp.

[49] *Ibid.,* ad 4um. One will find a masterpiece of theological exposition on this point in the *Compendium Theologiae*, Cap. 239, n. 514. We shall develop the meritorious aspect of Christ's satisfaction later when we come to the theology of the shedding of blood.

him up from the dead" (Rom 10:9).[50]

The Ascension

"To the light through the cross." St. Thomas applies in due proportion all that he has just taught about the Resurrection to the mystery of the Ascension.

> Christ, in ascending once for all into heaven, obtained for himself and for us for eternity the right and dignity of dwelling in heaven.[51]
>
> Christ's Passion is the cause of our ascent into heaven properly speaking because it removes the obstacle of sin and is meritorious. Christ's Ascension, on the other hand, is the cause of our ascent in so far as this Ascension, which has begun with him, our head, must now be extended to include us, the members of his body, who should be one with him *(quasi inchoando ipsam in capite nostro cui oportet membra coniungi).*[52]

Once he has expounded in the body of this article of the *Summa Theologica* the great value of the Ascension in so far as it engages us personally in the mystery of the redemption (through the practice of our faith, hope and love, and, also, through our reverence for Jesus, who is no longer thought of as an "earthly man" but as "heavenly God") St. Thomas goes on to show how the Ascension is the cause of our salvation objectively: Jesus has shown us the way, he is our head, and where the head is there the members must follow. "I am going to prepare a home for you . . . so that you

---

[50] *Comm. in 2 Tim.* 2, lect. 2, n. 49.

[51] IIIa, qu. 57, art. 6, ad 3um.

[52] *Ibid.*, ad 2um.

too may be where I am" (John 14:2–3). Just as the high priest in Old Testament times entered the sanctuary to pray to God on behalf of the people, so also has Christ "entered heaven to intercede for us" (Heb 7:25). By reason of his human nature he is in heaven as a living intercession for us, and the Father takes pity on those for whom his Son became man. As their master and Lord in the kingdom of heaven, Jesus distributes God's gifts to mankind.[53]

It follows that the Ascension must be thought of together with the sitting at the Father's right hand ("sitting" in the sense of "being seated"; this signifies the royalty and omnipotence of the Savior).

Because Jesus is God he enjoys the same glory, the same happiness and the same royal power as his Father.[54] As man, Christ "enjoys possession of the divine riches in a more excellent way than any other creature,"[55] and distributes them abundantly among the members of his Mystical Body.

> "Molded into the pattern of his death" (Phil 3:10), we are led on to immortal glory; as the Apostle says, "if we are his children, then we are his heirs too; heirs of God, sharing the inheritance of Christ; only we must share his sufferings, if we are to share his glory" (Rom 8:17).[56]
>
> To God alone does it belong to make souls happy by their participation in himself; but the leading of souls to happiness belongs to Christ as their head and the originator of their salvation; as

---

[53] *Ibid.*, art. 6.
[54] See IIIa, qu. 58, art. 2.
[55] *Ibid.*, art. 4.
[56] See IIia, qu. 49, art. 3, ad 3um.

we read in the Epistle to the Hebrews: "But we can see this: we can see one who was made a little lower than the angels, I mean Jesus, crowned now with glory and honor because of the death he underwent; in God's gracious design he was to taste death, and to taste it on behalf of all. . . . It befitted the majesty of God that, in summoning all those sons of his to glory, he should crown with suffering the life of that Prince who was to lead them into salvation. The Son who sanctifies and the sons who are sanctified have a common origin, all of them"[57] (2:9–11).[58]

Christ the Redeemer will be all in all for ever in the kingdom of heaven: "The saints in heaven will have no further need of Christ's atonement; nevertheless, although their atonement be over, they will always need (*indigebunt*, 'be needy,' like beggars) to be consummated by Christ *(consummari per ipsum Christum)* on whom their glory depends. For this reason we read in Revelation: 'Nor had the city any need of sun or moon to shew in it; the glory of God shone there, and the Lamb gave it light'" (21:23).[59]

---

[57] Here the Bible of Jerusalem adds a note to its translation: "The context would also allow one to translate: 'He who sanctifies and those who are sanctified form a single whole.'" Clearly these two possible translations are complementary. The second has the advantage of expressing better the doctrine of the Mystical Body.

[58] IIIa, qu. 59, art. 2, ad 2um.

[59] IIIa, qu. 22, art. 5, ad 1um. See Fr. Lyonnet's article, "La Valeur soteriologique du Christ selon Saint Paul," in *Gregorianum*, 2, 295–318 (1958): F. X. Durrwell, *La resurrection de Jésus, mystere de salut* (Paris, 1955), English translation by Rosemary Sheed, *The Resurrection* (London, 1960); L. Cerfaux, *Le Christ dans la théologie de Saint Paul* (Paris, 1951), English translation by G. Webb and A. Walker, *Christ in the Theology of St Paul* (New York, 1959).

CHAPTER III

VICARIOUS SATISFACTION: THE PREEMINENCE OF MERCY

The most beautiful death of love.
—St. Thérèse of Lisieux[1]

WE SHALL NOW CONSIDER THE MYSTERY of our redemption under the separate aspects of vicarious satisfaction, merit, redemption and sacrifice. These are not concepts of the kind that, "once duly enumerated, embrace a whole which exceeds the limitations of each taken separately; they are, if one may say so, concentric notions which are focused by reflection on a single object." One and the same principle sustains them all, which is "the love Christ displayed in his Passion."[2]

---

[1] *Novissima Verba*, July 4th.
[2] Rivière, *Le Dogme de la Rédemption*, 303 and 300.

THE CHURCH'S MAGISTERIUM

The following texts of the Church's Magisterium express the Catholic doctrine of Christ's satisfaction, called "vicarious satisfaction," for the sins of mankind. The Council of Ephesus in 431 states solemnly in a canon: "If any man say that the Word Incarnate offered himself as a sacrifice for himself and not rather for us (for he who knew no sin had no need of sacrifice), let him be anathema."[3]

The Council of Trent in the sixteenth century reiterates this doctrine: "If any man assert that original sin can be taken away by any remedy other than the merit of the one mediator, our Lord Jesus Christ, who reconciled us to God in his blood, became 'our justification, our sanctification, and our atonement' (1 Cor 1:30) . . . , let him be anathema."[4] "The meritorious cause (of our justification) is the most beloved Son of God, our Lord Jesus Christ, who, when we were his enemies, because of the surpassing love with which he loved us, merited justification for us and made satisfaction to the Father by his most sacred Passion on the wood of the cross."[5]

The Roman Catechism treats of our subject at length:

> The preaching of the mystery of our Lord's Passion should be the especial object of our careful study so that the faithful, moved by the remembrance of such a benefaction, may turn to God with all their heart to receive the outpouring of his love and kindness. . . . The Christian religion rests upon

---

[3] Canon X, Denz. 122.
[4] Sess. V, *Decretum super Peccatum Originale*, Denz. 790.
[5] Sess. VI, cap. 7, Denz. 799.

this article of faith as upon its foundation, and, this foundation once assured, all the remaining truths can be seen in their true perspective. The mystery of the cross is the most difficult mystery of all, and we are scarcely able to grasp that our salvation should depend on the cross of one who was nailed to its wood for our sakes. Nevertheless, together with the Apostle, we may there admire the most striking manifestation of divine providence. . . . Jesus Christ did not act against his will, he was under no compulsion, he offered himself because he so desired, and accepted spontaneously the torments so cruelly and unjustly inflicted on him. . . . Thus did Christ give us evidence of the profoundest and most precious charity. . . . Why did Christ desire his suffering to be so extreme? He wished to redeem us, to wipe out the sins of all time, and to make total and abundant satisfaction for us before his Father. . . . The Father delivered up his Son: "Be sure it is for my people's guilt I have smitten him" (Isa 53:8), "God laid on his shoulders our guilt, the guilt of us all" *(ibid.* 6) . . . . The Apostle has expressed the same truth still more strongly in his desire to show, from another point of view, with how much reason we should hope in the immense mercy of divine goodness. "He did not even spare his own Son, but gave him up for us all; and must not that gift be accompanied by the gift of all else?" (Rom 8:32). . . . Christ has expiated the punishments due to us for our sins. He has reconciled us with his Father, appeased him, and caused him to be propitious to us. He has abolished the sins of the world. . . . This, Christ's satisfaction for our sins, was not merely adequate, but it was superabundant. His sacrifice on the altar of the cross was as pleasing as possible to God, whose anger and indignation he appeased completely, as the Apostle says to the Ephesians: "Order your lives in charity, upon the model of that charity which Christ shewed to us, when he gave himself up on our behalf, a sacrifice breathing out fragrance as he offered it to God" (5:2).[6]

The drafts of the Vatican Council which concern the redemption were neither adopted nor promulgated, due to the sudden interruption of that Council; but they possess, nonetheless, great doctrinal authority as witnessing to the faith of the Fathers there assembled. We read in them:

> Jesus Christ, the mediator of God and men, in dying alone for all, has truly satisfied divine justice on our behalf. If death has reigned through one man, with how much more reason will they who receive the great abundance of grace, pardon and justice, possess the kingdom of life through the one Jesus Christ (Rom 5:17).[7]
>
> If any man presume to state that the vicarious satisfaction of a single mediator for all men is repugnant to the divine justice, let him be anathema.
>
> If any man fail to confess that the Word of God himself was able to make satisfaction, or that he has

---

[6] *Catechismus Romanus,* pars. Ia, cap. 5, nn. 1, 5, 7, 11, 14, 15. An interpretation in terms of the Father's anger with the Son is excluded by the context.

[7] *Constitutio Dogmatica de Fide Catholica,* cap. IV. See Richard, 185–9.

not really and properly made that satisfaction for our sins in suffering and dying in the flesh he assumed— not confess, moreover, that he has thus merited grace and glory for us, let him be anathema.[8]

Pius XII, in his Encyclical *Humani generis* of 1950, warned against perversion of the notions of original sin, of sin in general, considered as an offence against God, and of satisfaction such as was made by our Savior.[9]

The same pope's Encyclical *Haurietis aquas* of 1956, concerning the Sacred Heart, is more explicit:

> The mystery of our divine Redeemer is fundamentally and essentially a mystery of love; the mystery, namely, of that love of Christ for his heavenly Father by which he offers him the sacrifice of the cross in a spirit of love and obedience and achieves the superabundant and infinite satisfaction which was due through the faults of mankind. . . . This is, besides, the mystery of the merciful love for all men of the august Trinity and the divine Redeemer. . . . This is the reason why the divine Redeemer, in as much as he was the rightful and perfect mediator and redressed through his burning love the balance between the duties and debts of mankind and the exigencies of God's justice, has undoubtedly achieved the wonderful conciliation of divine mercy and justice in which the absolute transcendence of the mystery of our salvation is truly to be found.[10]

---

[8] *Ibid.*, canons 5 and 6.
[9] See Denz. 2318.
[10] *Acta Apostolicae Sedis*, 48 (1956), 321–2.

Rivière has accurately appraised the doctrinal value of the phrase, "vicarious satisfaction": "Though it lacks the canonical authority of a term defined by the Church," he writes, "the concept of vicarious satisfaction does really belong to the Catholic formulation of the dogma of the redemption."[11]

NO RETRIBUTIVE JUSTICE

God the Father did not exercise the right of retributive justice either on Christ himself or on sinners in his person. Therefore, Christ's sufferings are not punishments. This was clearly seen by St. Thomas and he does not labor the point only because it seems to him self-evident. This highly important, if negative, detail of doctrine deserves to hold our attention a little longer.

St. Thomas' thought can be reduced to this: it would be both cruel and unjust to punish an innocent man in the place of a felon; but Christ was innocence itself; hence it is inconceivable that he should suffer and die in our place to satisfy a just revenge. He could not be the object of the Father's wrath.[12]

It would be both cruel and unjust to punish an innocent man in the place of a felon.

In commenting on the words of St. Paul, "The powers we have are used in support of the truth, not against it" (2 Cor 13:8), St Thomas writes: "It is obvious that, were we to punish the innocent, we should be violating all truth and justice. The Apostle cannot

---

[11] Rivière, *Le Dogme de la Rédemption*, 123.

[12] It must also be sufficiently evident that the Passion of anger is only attributed to God metaphorically. Properly speaking and analogically, we speak of God's anger when we wish to indicate his decision to impose just punishment for sin.

act contrary to the truth but only in support of it, that is, in support of justice, and so it is also plain that he will not punish the innocent."[13] "A man who moves against one who has done him some wrong does not appear wholly wicked, but, supposing this person has done him no wrong at all, then his wickedness is unrelieved."[14]

"He who kills an innocent person wrongs both God and society in addition to his victim, as is the case in suicide."[15]

What is at stake is the virtue of justice. "Where punishment for sin is to be imposed precisely as such, a man may only be punished for his own sin since the sinful act is a personal act."[16]

When an innocent man is punished he cannot be said to suffer directly from his fault, "he does suffer the pain of the penalty, and this is all the more acute for him because of his very innocence, in so far as he realizes its injustice. For this reason, also, others are the more to be blamed if they lack compassion for him."[17]

But Christ is not only innocent, he is innocence itself.

"Christ was, in an absolute sense, sinless,"[18] because he was God.

There are three reasons why Christ took on some of our weaknesses (such as hunger, thirst, exhaustion, sleep, acute pain): to satisfy for our sins, to emphasize the reality of his human nature, and to leave us an example of virtue. But sin could not have made sense

---

[13] *Comm. in 2 Cor.* 13, lect. 2, n. 531.

[14] *Comm. in Psalm.* 34, n. 5, 427.

[15] IIIa, qu. 47, art. 6, ad 3um.

[16] Ia IIae, qu. 87, art. 8.

[17] IIIa, qu. 46, art. 6, ad 5um.

[18] IIIa, qu. 22, art. 4, ad 1um.

in any of these ways; for sin, far from contributing towards it, is directly opposed to the making of satisfaction, as it is also opposed to human nature which has God for its author, and, again, to virtue, of which it is the contrary.[19]

Hence Christ could neither suffer nor die to satisfy retributive justice.

"The slayers of Christ cannot be excused from injustice,"[20] that is the final verdict.

For, as St. Thomas clearly and repeatedly states, Christ could never have contracted the debt which would have made him liable to suffering and death. "Christ in his Passion lowered himself far beneath the deserts of his dignity . . . by his suffering and death which he owed to no one to have to undergo."[21]

"His death was not due to sin."[22]

"Christ had not merited death since he was sinless."[23]

"Christ, since he was not subject to sin, was liable neither to death nor corruption, but accepted death voluntarily for our salvation."[24]

"Christ accepted death of his own free will in order to make satisfaction for us and not as though bound by the penalty for original sin, for he was not liable to

[19] IIIa, qu. 15, art. 1 corp. "Christ lacked the sensual inclination to sin (*fomes peccati*) because the more perfect a man's virtue the less is he inclined to sin; but Christ was possessed of consummate virtue" (*ibid.*, art. 2 corp.). "Christ, in extinguishing completely all desires of the flesh antagonistic to the spirit, gave evidence of fortitude in the highest degree" (*ibid.*, ad 3um).
[20] IIIa, qu. 47, art. 6, ad 3um.
[21] IIIa, qu. 49, art. 6.
[22] IIIa, qu. 51, art. 4 corp.
[23] IIIa, qu. 49, art. 2.
[24] IIIa, qu. 51, art. 3, ad 1um.

death (*ipse mortis debitor non erat*)."[25]

"It was fitting for Christ to descend into hell, not because he was liable to punishment, but in order to free those who were."[26]

Strictly speaking, the cause of Christ's death was not sin at all, neither his, for he had none, nor ours, but his love for the Father and for us on the occasion of our sins.[27]

For these reasons it is advisable to avoid using the analogy of the innocent hostage to illustrate Christ our Redeemer's vicarious satisfaction. He who freely volunteered to take the place of one condemned to death would certainly die a victim of his own charity. He would have saved the condemned man either, supposing he were innocent, from the execution of violence following upon a tyrannical verdict, or, supposing he were a felon, from the just consequences of a reasonable verdict.

---

[25] IIIa, qu. 35, art. 6, ad 1um.

[26] IIIa, qu. 52, art. 1, ad 1um.

[27] See *Comm. in Joan.* 14, lect. 8, nn. 1974–6. The *efficient cause* is that which is directly and positively responsible for the effect and that to which the effect is said to owe its origin. The occasion is, positively, a circumstance allowing the cause to operate effectively; negatively, it is a circumstance which obstructs its operation. For example: the turning on of a tap is the *occasion* of a flow of water, but its *cause* is the pressure itself of the water (either due to its weight or for some other reason). Sin could not be the direct cause but only the occasion of our Lord's death. This distinction, though it may appear over-subtle at first glance, is fundamental in reality. For sin is powerless before Christ who is innocence itself. Hence St. Thomas is being theologically exact in saying that sin did not cause Christ's death. But one may still say and preach correctly that Christ died because of our sins, provided only that these words are correctly understood. The causality in question is indirect, that of an occasion.

In the former of these cases, to offer oneself as a substitute might be timely and would certainly be heroic. In the latter, such substitution would be unreasonable. But in either case, or in all similar cases, authority would be at fault in accepting the proposal to kill one who was innocent. This would be a loathsome murder, flying in the face of all justice.

But we are guilty sinners; Christ is innocence itself and divine authority, wise beyond comparison. Hence the claims of justice explain nothing here. If he who is innocent is condemned this is, objectively, a crime. Christ's butchers are the basest of police executioners and not priests in a sacrifice. They do not act in God's name, and Christ, their victim, is the victim of an injustice.

One cannot say, therefore, as does Mgr. d'Hulst, in the train of Luther and Calvin, that Christ became sin for us inasmuch as, "the divine mercy being set aside,"[28] he became the object of a divine punishment in our place in the interests of retributive justice. So understood, penal substitution would be, not a mystery, but a misrepresentation of justice in God, a bidding of defiance to morality, an out and out contradiction.[29]

SOME FUNDAMENTAL NOTIONS

Some fundamental notions such as sin, atonement and vicarious satisfaction have still to be analyzed.

---

[28] Maurice Le Sage d'Hauteroche d'Hulst, *Carême de 1891*, quoted by Rivière, *Le Dogme de la Rédemption*, 234.

[29] Christ's vicarious satisfaction only becomes comprehensible in the light, first of all, of love, and then of loving justice, mercy playing always a paramount part. See *Etudes Carmelitaines, loc. cit.*, 105–25.

Sin and atonement

God is dishonored when the sinner disobeys him and turns inordinately to creaturely good. The sinner violates God's law when he disturbs the order which God wills. From God's point of view, sin is an offence and an affront to his honor. From that of the sinner, it is a fault which is said, metaphorically, to stain his soul: "The soul stains itself in clinging inordinately to goods less than God because, in so doing, it acts against the light of reason and the requirements of the divine law."[30]

The way to atone for this offence and purify oneself of this moral stain lies through conversion and satisfaction.[31]

First of all conversion. Sanctity comes about through union with God, and this union belongs to the will moved by grace. The sinner must, therefore, break with the wrong attachment, which binds him to creatures, in order to turn back to God. To do this he should lovingly accept the order of divine justice.[32] This return to God is his conversion.

But he who has sinned deserves to be punished. A reason for this, given by St. Thomas, goes to the heart of the matter: "Only punishment can repair the disorder of sin and restore it to the order of justice. For it is right that he who has unduly indulged his own willfulness should suffer something he does not will; in this way a just equilibrium is regained *(sic erit aequalitas).*[33] "Satisfaction involves punishment as a compensation

---

[30] Ia IIae, qu. 86, art. 1, ad 1um.
[31] See IIIa, qu. 89 art. 3 corp.
[32] See Ia IIae, qu. 87, art. 6 corp.
[33] IIIa, qu. 86, art. 4 corp.

for the pleasure wrongfully taken in sin."[34] "It is essential to punishment to be against the will of him who suffers it."[35]

The guilty person may or may not accept his punishment,[36] and here St. Thomas distinguishes between punishment *qua* punishment and punishment *qua* satisfaction. The former is inflicted on the sinner for as long as he fails to accept it willingly; the latter is, on the contrary, accepted willingly in view of the requirements of divine justice *vis-à-vis* a sin already repented.

Here it is most important to grasp the fundamental principle that it is not punishment but love which makes satisfaction what it is essentially. It is the loving acceptance of punishment for the love of God which gives it whatever value of satisfaction it may possess.

"Satisfaction which did not proceed from charity would be ineffectual."[37]

"A man is said to make satisfaction strictly speaking for an offence when he offers the offended person something he loves as much as or more than he hated the offence."[38]

"What matters most in making satisfaction is the good intention (*affectus*) of him who offers it, not the quality of his offering."[39]

---

[34] *De Veritate*, qu. 26, art. 6, ad 4um in contr.

[35] Ia IIae, qu. 87, art. 2 corp. Punishments are called "retributive" in so far as they allow the sinner to atone for his sins as offences against God; "medicinal and purifying" in so far as they should contribute to his sanctification. These two points of view are distinct and *mutually complementary.*

[36] See Ia IIae, qu. 87, art. 6 corp.

[37] IIIa, qu. 14, art. 1, ad 1um.

[38] IIIa, qu. 48, art. 2 corp.

[39] IIIa, qu. 79, art. 5.

"It is charity which makes works of satisfaction pleasing to God. Lacking charity they lack all value as satisfaction."[40]

Punishment is desirable since it atones for sinful enjoyment as well as strengthening and giving concrete form to our repentance. Punishment enables the whole man to do penance, but, in the last analysis, it is worth no more and no less than the love with which it is accepted and endured. Sufferings cordially embraced are the signs and instruments of love (and of contrition in the case of a sinner). The stronger a man's love, the greater his capacity to suffer. Difficulty, when well and truly faced, is a sign, an occasion and an instrument of merit, but the only true cause of merit is love, "for our Lord does not care so much for the importance of our works as for the love with which they are done."[41]

This fundamental principle of the supreme importance of love in works of satisfaction has, also, a moral application of the greatest value which may be formulated thus: the greater the purity and fervour of love the less does punishment become necessary and desirable for the sake of mere justice, until the point is reached where satisfaction may be totally accomplished by and in the intensity of love. Love and punishment stand in an inverse ratio to one another:

> We should take into account that, when a soul turns away from sin, its disgust for sin and its adhesion to God may be so vehement that there will remain

---

[40] IIIa (supplementum), qu. 14, art. 2.
[41] St. Teresa of Avila, *The Interior Castle*, 292 (translation of the Benedictines of Stanbrook, London, 1912). See *Etudes Carmelitaines, loc. cit.,* 112.

no further obligation to undergo punishment. . . . The necessity of suffering satisfactory and purgative punishment may be excluded by the vehemence both of love for God and of loathing for past sin; and, even when this vehemence is not such as will exclude punishment totally, nevertheless, the greater the vehemence the less the degree of punishment needed to suffice.[42] [This is so true that] the greater the dignity of him who atones, the greater the punishment he suffers is held to be, because it is accompanied by a correspondingly greater degree of humility and charity.[43]

Psychologically, also, it is true that the more one loves the less one labours: "Love takes away labor, or, if labor there be, that labor is itself loved."[44] The psychological relief found in the love of charity makes no difference to the moral efficacy of the satisfaction made.[45]

The preeminence of love in satisfaction is a doctrine which is uniformly coherent and thoroughly optimistic.

No anthropomorphism

Satisfaction is the repayment of a debt. In the sphere of human relations this claim of justice may be of a *real* or of a *personal* nature. It is a real claim if I have injured

---

[42] *Contra Gentiles*, III, cap. 158.

[43] *Ibid.*, IV, cap. 55, ad 23um.

[44] St. Augustine is often quoted in this form: *Ubi amatur non laboratur, aut si laboratur labor amatur.* Cf. *In eo quod amatur, aut non laboratur, aut et labor amatur* (*De Bono Viduitatis*, 21, 26: *P.L.* 40, col. 448).

[45] See IIIa (suppl.), qu. 15, art. 1, ad 2um.

someone in his possessions, and I am then bound to make restitution. It is a personal claim if I have injured his reputation, in which case I am bound to make reparation. This may possibly take the form of an indemnification in money but, even so, it will not, strictly speaking, be restitution but will remain in the line of reparation or atonement.

In our relations with God we are never strictly bound to make restitution since sin can do nothing to diminish his infinite perfection; but by sin we do offend God where his providential government is concerned, and both wrong him and obscure his rights in so far as we can. It is already clear, however, that commutative justice does not govern our relations with God nor his with us. "Satisfaction is made to God . . . restitution is made to our neighbor."[46]

Some texts from Scripture and St. Thomas will help to illustrate this point: "See the children gathering sticks, the father lighting a fire, the mother kneading dough, and all to make cakes for the queen of heaven! See how they offer libation to alien gods, to despite me! Yet not to me they do despite, the Lord says, rather to themselves" (Jer 7:18–19).

"Look heavenward, mark how the skies tower above thee, and read thy lesson there. Multiply thy wrong-doing as thou wilt, no sin of thine can harm or touch him; be honest as the day, no gift thou makest him, he is none the richer for thy pains. Only to thy fellow man thy malice does a hurt; only Adam's children profit by thy uprightness" (Job 35:5–8).

"Thy wickedness may hurt a man that is like thee: and thy justice may help the son of man" *(ibid.* verse 8).

---

[46] *IV Sent.,* dist. 15, qu. 1, art. 5, art. 1, sed contr.

As St. Thomas writes so profoundly: "God is never offended by us save in so far as we act in opposition to our own good."[47] Hence, if we were to make any *restitution* strictly speaking, we should have to make it by returning to ourselves the true good of which we had deprived ourselves for the sake of an apparent good.

But though there is nothing, and for good reasons, which we have to restore to God, the duty of offering him satisfaction still remains; for we have really and seriously offended him. This point of view may be meditated upon in the following texts:

It is not that man really damages God when he sins against him, but he does deny him that which he owes him and diminishes his glory in so far as he is able, even though he cannot do so really.[48] Though nothing can be taken from God as he is in himself, the sinner does, nevertheless, deny him something by his sin in so far as this lies in his power.[49] Though the sinner can in no way effectively harm God by his sin, he antagonizes God on his own side in two ways, namely: he scorns God in his commandments; he harms either himself or his neighbor, which is not without some bearing on God since we are all beneath the protection of his providence.[50] By his acts man can neither add anything to God nor subtract anything from him as he is in himself; yet man can, so far as in him lies, offer something to God or deny him something by

---

[47] *Contra Gentiles*, III, cap. 122.
[48] *II Sent.*, dist. 42, qu. 2, art. 2, sol. 2, ad 1um.
[49] *IV Sent.*, dist. 15, qu. 1, art. 4, sol. 1.
[50] Ia IIae, qu. 47, art. 1, ad 1um.

observing or failing to observe the order God has instituted.[51]

In short, God precisely because he is God, does not employ an accountant to demand restitution before he himself gives back his friendship. There is nothing we can restore to him which he has not first of all given to us. There is neither conversion nor satisfaction without charity, and charity is the fruit *par excellence* of divine mercy. Our duty to make atonement for sin contributes to both the glory of God and our own personal advantage: the man who atones and makes satisfaction here on earth purifies himself and grows in love while making himself ready to sing the divine mercies in eternity. The task which he accomplishes is one of both justice and love, but primarily of love.[52]

---

[51] Ia IIae, qu. 21, art. 4, ad 1um. Cf. P. Joseph Lecuyer, "Note sur une définition thomiste de la satisfaction," in *Doctor Communis*, I (1955), 21–30. These and other quotations will be found in this article which we have been following closely here.

[52] At the opposite extreme the condemned soul, which unceasingly renews its rebellion against God, makes itself the victim of a retributive justice totally devoid of love. It is not that the condemned fail to glorify God; they do indeed glorify him, but in everlasting unhappiness and in spite of themselves. Satisfaction is not possible in hell.

The soul in purgatory does expiate its faults. Purification is the primary end envisaged by its sufferings which are the consequences of both God's and the soul's justice and love, with love predominating for both.

Absolutely speaking, God desires directly neither hell nor purgatory for anyone since he does not desire sin. All should die fully purified of their faults and the penalties due to them, and with the faith, confidence and love won for us by the merits of our Lord Jesus Christ; they could then, as St. Thérèse of Lisieux puts it, "fling themselves without hindrance [that is, without passing through purgatory] into the eternal embrace of merciful love." "One receives as much as one hopes for," as St. John of the Cross

Vicarious satisfaction

St. Thomas states clearly: "The sinner alone may be punished for his sin when it is a question of inflicting punishment precisely as such," for then it is a question of justice; but, "when a penalty is freely undergone in order to make satisfaction one man may take the place of another";[53] such a man is then a volunteer spontaneously performing an act of charity. An example would be the benefactor who pays the fine incurred by a pauper: the law would have no power to compel him to do this, but he would respect justice for love of the pauper.

In the same way, one satisfies for the sin of another when one freely suffers the penalty due to his sin.[54] And this is vicarious satisfaction: the sufferings undergone furnish the material element while compassionate love for the guilty person is the principle which makes the material element efficacious.[55]

But two conditions must be fulfilled: firstly, there must be a natural or moral link between the guilty person and the person making satisfaction for the fault;[56] secondly, this solidarity of the two together must be accepted by the person offended.[57]

---

says. See the work already quoted, *La doctrine de Sainte Therese de l'Enfant-Jésus sur le purgatoire*, and the article, "Épreuves Spirituelles" in the *Dictionnaire de Spiritualite.*

[53] Ia IIae, qu. 87, art. 8.

[54] See IIIa, qu. 14, art. 1 corp.

[55] See *Ibid.*, ad 1um. Sufferings undergone out of compassion for another's sin are retributive in character but are called "redemptive" sufferings, or sufferings of "merciful justice."

[56] See Ia IIae, qu. 87, art. 7 corp.

[57] These two points will be more strongly emphasized later on in discussing the *merit* of Christ's Passion.

Here the inverse ratio between love and suffering operates in favor of him who makes reparation:

> One man may make satisfaction for another pro-
> vided he has charity, without which no valid satis-
> faction is possible. Nor need one say, as some do,
> that a more intense suffering should be inflicted
> on him who makes satisfaction in such a case, the
> reason alleged being that the guilty man's suffer-
> ing is worth more than that of anybody else. This
> is untrue because suffering has its value of satis-
> faction in the first place from charity, and it is
> clear that greater charity is needed to satisfy for
> another than for oneself. Hence the least suffering
> of the innocent for the sake of the guilty may be
> enough.[58]

It would seem, therefore, that vicarious satisfaction envisages the fulfilment of justice in virtue
of merciful love while ensuring that he who makes
it should not be liable to an infliction of retributive
justice by the person offended. Strictly speaking, one
might still speak of penal substitution provided one
abandoned the more usual pejorative sense we have
criticized above. But to avoid misunderstandings it
seems preferable to abandon the term "substitution"
altogether and use "solidarity" in its place.[59]

This concept of vicarious satisfaction is the fruit

---

[58] IIIa (Suppl.), qu. 13, art 2.

[59] See Fr. Lyonnet, "La soteriologie paulinienne" in *Introduction a la
Bible* (under the direction of A. Robert and A. Feuillet), II (Paris,
1959), 876: "It has been seen for a long time now that the favorite
formula (of St. Paul) was not 'instead of' but 'for the sake of' in
conformity with the usual meaning of this Greek preposition when
governing a personal noun," etc.

of a theological elaboration of the dogma of redemption. It does, in fact, seem to be the most accurate way of expressing this profound mystery. St. Thomas often gives the substance of it. "Christ suffered a penalty in satisfaction for our sins and not for any of his own."[60] "Christ suffered for us what we had deserved to suffer ourselves as a consequence of the sin of our first parents, and first of all death, which crowns all human sufferings. Thus Christ wished to suffer death for our sakes so as to be able to free us from (spiritual) death: this he did by accepting, in spite of his innocence, the punishment due to us."[61]

Christ was *marvelously suited to make such satisfaction since he was both God and man. As man*, he possessed as material for satisfaction a passible and mortal body; *as God made man*, he possessed a heart burning with charity for his Father and for us, with that charity which gives the work of expiation all its value.[62]

It is most important to remember that this vicarious satisfaction involves both justice and mercy together, and that it is only in the interests of analysis that we deal with each separately in the reflections which follow.

---

[60] Ia IIae, qu. 87, art. 7, ad 3um. The phrase itself, "vicarious satisfaction," is not to be found in St. Thomas.

[61] *Compendium Theologiae*, cap. 227, n. 475.

[62] See IIIa, qu. 14, art. 1, ad 1um.

JESUS CHRIST IS THE VICTIM OF LOVE

In union with his Father

Jesus tells his disciples that "the Son of Man must be given up to be crucified," but he does not say who will give him up.

His Father gave him up: "He did not even spare his own Son, but gave him up for us all" (Rom 8:32). And he gave himself up: "That charity which Christ showed to us, when he gave himself up on our behalf" (Eph 5:2). And Judas gave him up: "What will you pay me for handing him over to you?" (Matt 26:15). He was given up, also, to Pilate by the Jews: "It is thy own nation, and its chief priests, who have given thee up to me" (John 18:35). And, finally, Pilate gave him up to the gentiles: "Thereupon he gave Jesus up into their hands to be crucified" (John 19:16).[63]

This "giving up" may be taken in a good or a bad sense according to circumstances and intentions. "The Father gave up Christ and Christ gave up himself through love, and hence they are praised for it: but Judas gave up Christ out of cupidity, the Jews out of envy, and Pilate out of human respect because he feared Caesar, and therefore they are blamed for it."[64]

Christ said: "This my Father loves in me, that I am laying down my life, to take it up again afterwards. Nobody can rob me of it; I lay it down of my own accord. I am free to lay it down, free to take it up again; that is the charge which my Father has given me" (John 10:17–18). And St. John Chrysostom here

---

[63] *Comm. in Matt.* 26, n. 2121.
[64] IIIa, qu. 47, art. 3, ad 3um.

observes that Jesus wished to emphasize the voluntary nature of his Passion and remove any suspicion that he was opposed to his Father's will.[65]

St. Thomas explains how the Father can be thought of as delivering up his Son: God had predestined Christ's Passion from all eternity for the liberation of mankind; he inspired in him the desire to suffer for us by infusing charity in him; finally he did not protect him from suffering, but left him exposed to his persecutors.[66]

After clearly reaffirming that "it is impious and cruel to give up an innocent man to suffering and death against his will," St. Thomas continues,

> but God the Father did not give up Christ in this way; rather he inspired in him the desire to suffer voluntarily for our sakes.[67]
>
> Christ, as God, gave himself up to death with the same wish and act as the Father had in giving him up; but, as man, he gave himself up through a desire inspired in him by the Father. Hence there is no opposition arising from the fact that both the Father gave up Christ and Christ gave up himself.[68]
>
> It was neither impious nor cruel of God to wish Christ's death. He did not compel him as though it were against his will, but was pleased by the charity which caused Christ to accept his death. And it was he who infused this charity into his soul.[69]

---

[65] See *Ibid.*, art. 2, ad 1um.
[66] See *Ibid.*, art. 3 corp.
[67] *Ibid.*, ad 1um.
[68] *Ibid.*, ad 2um.
[69] *Contra Gentiles*, IV, cap. 55, ad 16um.

The decisive and determining motive for Christ's Passion is nothing less than the surpassing love of charity of which he, together with his Father, wished to give us evidence in the human nature he had freely assumed. On the one hand, and quite independently of original sin, this human nature is perfectly capable of suffering and death, for this is its normal condition; on the other, "this is the greatest love a man can show, that he should lay down his life for his friends" (John 15:13), and Christ wished to give this sign of the greatest love to the whole human race. In order to give it even more strikingly, he wished to die in the prime of life, in full and perfect vigor;[70] and yet Christ's bodily life was of such great dignity, because, above all, of the divinity to which it was united, that he suffered more in losing it than any other man could possibly have done.[71]

Through obedience

"He lowered his own dignity, accepted an obedience which brought him to death, death on a cross" (Phil 2:8). Obedience is the mark of humility, a way of humbling oneself; it is the proud, on the contrary, who follow their own wills and pursue their own aggrandizement in order to be beholden to no one and to domineer at their pleasure. Obedience is incompatible with pride. It is, in the last analysis, dependence and submission to God. As Jesus said to Pilate: "Thou wouldst not have any power over me at all, if it had not been given thee from above" (John 19:11).

It is because the Apostle wishes to exalt Christ's

---

[70] See IIIa, qu. 46, art. 9, ad 4um.
[71] See *Ibid.*, art. 6, ad 4um.

humility in his Passion that he tells us he accepted an obedience, for this is a claim of our Lord's to still greater merit. But how could Christ accept an obedience? Certainly it was not as God, the supreme ruler, that he did so, but as man, wishing to carry out in everything the will of his Father to whom he would say without ceasing: "only as thy will is, not as mine is" (Matt 26:39).

It is all the more important to speak of obedience in connection with the Passion since the first sin was one of disobedience: "A multitude will become acceptable to God through one man's obedience, just as a multitude, through one man's disobedience, became guilty" (Rom 5:19).

How marvellous Christ's obedience is! It is no small thing to antagonize one's own desires because one obeys, and everyone desires life and honor; yet Christ did not refuse to die the very death of the cross, the most shameful of all deaths (*ignominiosissima*): "It was thus that Christ died as a ransom, paid once for all, on behalf of our sins, he the innocent for us the guilty, so as to present us in God's sight" (1 Pet 3:18).[72] "Son of God though he was, he learned obedience in the school of suffering" (Heb 5:8). As the Son of God from all eternity, Christ could neither suffer nor feel compassion, and so he took the human nature which would make this possible for him. But how could this be possible? Only the ignorant have to learn; but Christ was God from all eternity and possessed as man the fullness of infused knowledge; he had nothing to learn.

---

[72] See *Comm. in Philip.* 2, lect. 2, n. 65; see also IIIa, qu. 47, art. 2 corp.

We must be careful, however. For there are two types of knowledge, one being exclusively theoretical (that of *simplicis notitiae*)—which is the type which is making the difficulty—the other practical or experimental *(scientia experientiae)*. It is in the context of this second type that Christ as man is said to have learnt the meaning of obedience from his sufferings. He obeyed in the most trying and difficult circumstances until his death on the cross (Phil 2:8).

The man who has never had to practice obedience in the face of difficulties thinks it an easy matter. Experience teaches one better. The person who has never practiced obedience will never make a good leader. Christ preached by example.[73] Christ is the perfect model of obedience.

A loving obedience

St. Thomas replies to the objection that Christ's Passion is to be attributed to his charity rather than to his obedience by saying, "It comes to the same thing, since Christ fulfilled the precepts of charity through obedience and obeyed his Father out of love."[74] And again, "Christ was obedient because it was in carrying out the command of his Father that he suffered death for our salvation (Phil 2:8). This is not to deny that Christ died out of love (Eph 5:2) since his obedience was the consequence of his love for the Father and for us."[75]

The two statements are, therefore, perfectly harmonious: Christ died for love *and* Christ died for obedience. The depth and interest of this teaching will be

---

[73] See *Comm. in Hebr.* 5, lect. 2, n. 259.
[74] IIIa, qu. 47, art. 2, ad 3um.
[75] *Comm. in Rom.* 5, lect. 5, n. 446.

more fully grasped if we recall St. Thomas' teaching concerning the place obedience occupies in the hierarchy of the virtues and its connection with charity. Is obedience the most perfect of the virtues?

The theological virtues come first since they effect union with God; next come the moral virtues which enable us to set aside the goods of this life in order to unite ourselves with God. But it is more important to be detached from the goods of the soul than from the goods of the body, as it is to be detached from the latter when compared with exterior goods; but the will is, as it were, the foremost good of the soul since it enables man to use all the rest. Thus obedience is foremost among moral virtues because it enables us to reject our own will for the sake of God. As St. Gregory says: "Obedience is truly considered to be more valuable than sacrifices because when one immolates a victim it is some other flesh that one immolates, but in the case of obedience it is one's own will." And this important consequence follows, namely, that the acts of no matter which virtue will only be meritorious before God in so far as they are performed in a spirit of obedience to his will. Were a man to suffer martyrdom or to distribute all his property to the poor and yet fail to order his activity upon an apprehension of the divine will, and this he would do through obedience, he would merit nothing and it would be exactly as though he had acted without charity, a virtue inseparable from obedience. For charity means friendship between God and ourselves, and friendship implies but a single will.[76]

---

[76] See IIa, IIae, qu. 104, art. 3 corp., and qu. 23, art. 1.

The precepts men receive from God concern works of virtue, and the more perfectly one performs such acts the more obedient one is to God. But charity is the foremost among the virtues, to which all the others are referred. And so Christ, whose act of charity was the most perfect possible, was supremely obedient to God. For there is no act of charity more perfect than that a man lay down his life for another, as our Lord himself says: "This is the greatest love a man can shew, that he should lay down his life for his friends" (John 15:13). And so it is that Christ, who suffered death for the salvation of men and the glory of God the Father, was supremely obedient through an act of perfect charity.[77]

In perfect freedom

Christ's enemies had often wished to arrest him in order to condemn him to death but they failed because his hour had not yet come (John 7:30, 44; 8:20; 10:39). The prince of this world could do nothing against him

---

[77] *Contra Gentiles,* IV, cap. 55, ad 3um. As Fr. Karl Rahner puts it so well: "What is the flesh but weakness, and fragility, being destined for death, the dimension of the appearance and the sensible manifestation of sin. It is the essential reality of man inasmuch as he has been a creature of flesh from the beginning, but situated in a free history, in his primordial history. The Logos took the 'flesh of sin'... the redemption was accomplished precisely in this dimension of man's existence, which could be at once that of the historical manifestation of his personal fault *and* that of the overcoming of this fault."

"One must try to think of death as both the co-natural manifestation of man's estrangement from God ... and as the manifestation and constitutive sign of absolute obedience to God..." K. Rahner, *Schriften zur Théologie,* I (Einsiedeln, 1954), 216, 217.

(John 14:30), and still the Scripture was to be fulfilled (John 19:28). The Good Shepherd gave his life for his sheep in perfect freedom, at a moment of his own choosing. "This my Father loves in me that I am laying down my life, to take it up again afterwards . . . . This is the charge which my Father has given me" (John 10:17–18). These statements leave no room for doubt: Christ submitted himself freely for love of his Father's command. Nevertheless, some theologians since St. Thomas have thought it impossible to maintain at the same time and unreservedly, both that Christ was incapable of sin and that he could submit himself freely to the command to die on the cross. Their fundamental difficulty may be summarized as follows: the man who submits himself freely to a command can fail to obey; but failure to obey means to sin; therefore, he can sin. Hence, supposing that Christ received and freely obeyed a command, he must have been able to sin. There follow various attempts to solve the problem.[78]

But we shall be able to dispense with this false problem and its equally false solutions if we return to St. Thomas' doctrine concerning the relationship between liberty and the capacity for sin. To be able to sin is to be able to turn away from the ultimate moral end, and this is a defect of liberty, the perfec-

---

[78] For Billot, Christ received no command strictly speaking. For Petau, he received a real command but one that was subject to dispensation or else, as Suarez and Vasquez maintain, that merely concerned the fact of death and not its painful circumstances. Such statements have no ground in Scripture, and the last two seem excessively artificial. Other authors, finally, seek to reconcile Christ's impeccability with a certain freedom to sin—a real squaring of the circle.

tion of which lies, on the contrary, in the power to choose this or that particular good in view of the last end. Thus the good angels and the blessed, who can no longer sin, enjoy a more perfect freedom of will than we who can still sin. Such perfection does not exclude the free choice of this or that particular good but only the free choice of sin.[79] Christ was incapable of sin because he was sovereignly and perfectly free, like the blessed who rejoice in the beatific vision. St. Thomas saw no special problem from this point of view in the fact that he received a command from his Father to die on the cross: "The obligation to obey is only opposed to freedom in the case of one who is averse to what is commanded"[80]; but this was not the case of Christ.

"The commandment of love is not opposed to freedom because it is only fulfilled willingly."[81] But the command to die on the cross commanded love; it was given by the Father for love of us and accepted by the Son for love of his Father and for us. It could only, then, be obeyed willingly, with love's own freedom.

---

[79] The same doctrine fundamentally is applied to the obligation of vows. To the objection: greater freedom means greater virtue; but the more one is bound by a vow the less one is free; therefore vows oppose virtue, St. Thomas replies: This objection is due to ignorance of the nature of necessity. There is, certainly, a necessity of compulsion which lessens merit because opposed to the exercise of free will; but there is also *a kind of* necessity which, in flowing from a voluntary inclination, far from diminishing merit, actually increases it. For the will then tends with greater intensity and freedom to the object of its love. The nearer one comes to perfection the more will one feel as though forced to act well, but always with complete liberty (*Contra Gentiles*, III, 139).

[80] IIa IIae, qu. 44, art. 1, ad 2um.

[81] *Ibid.*

WHAT IS REDEMPTION?

Rise Up, let us go on our way

"I have no longer much time for converse with you; one is coming, who has power over the world, but no hold over me. No, but the world must be convinced that I love the Father, and act only as the Father has commanded me to act. Rise up, we must be going on our way" (John 14:30–31). Our Lord wishes us to understand that the reason for his death should be a matter of consolation to us. For it is one thing to die because one has committed a crime—such a death might well give cause for sorrow—and quite another to die for duty or because of one's generosity in the practice of virtue—this kind of death is a source of consolation. "Let it not be said that any of you underwent punishment for murder, or theft . . . but, if a man is punished for being a Christian, he has no need to be ashamed of it" (1 Pet 4:15–16). But our Lord shows us, in this connection, that it is not our sins which have been the *cause* of his death,[82] but his own virtues of obedience and charity.

The prince of this world entered the heart of Judas to incite him to betray Christ, and into the hearts of the Jews that they might kill him; but he had no hold over Christ since Christ was innocent of sin. Sin was not the cause of his death. Was there, then, no reason for Christ's death? If we look elsewhere for the true cause of his death we find it in the twofold motive of love of God and love of neighbor.

Know, then, that I love my Father with an efficacious love. I die because that is his command. My obedience is caused by my love. The Father did not give this command

---

[82] They are only its occasion.

to the Word as such (for he is God with the Father), but to the Son of Man, that is, to the Word Incarnate, by inspiring him to die for man's salvation. So that the world may know that, let us go on our way from the supper to the place of my betrayal. Look and see: I do not die of necessity, but out of love and obedience.[83]

---

[83] See *Comm. in Joan.* 14, lect. 8, n. 1974–1976.

CHAPTER IV

VICARIOUS SATISFACTION AND MERCIFUL JUSTICE

When the Son of God tore himself from the Father's bosom for the salvation of men and suffered the humiliation of death, it was not justice which was constraining him.

—Paul Claudel[1]

JESUS CHRIST IS THE ATONEMENT FOR OUR SINS

The heart of the mystery

THE SACRIFICE OF PROPITIATION OR ATONEMENT makes God favorable to us (or propitious, hence its name); it restores our friendship with him: "Propitiation essentially implies compensation for wrongdoing, atoning for and remitting the guilt, and paying the penalty."[2]

---

[1] *L'Otage*, act 2, scene 2.
[2] La Taille, *Mysterium Fidei* (Paris, 1931), 319. English translation

WHAT IS REDEMPTION?

The mystery of redemption lies in the fact that it entails an act of divine justice in function of and wholly penetrated by divine mercy. We must neither exclude justice (the thesis of liberal theology) nor include it under the aspect of revenge (the thesis of the reformers, Luther and Calvin). Christ atoned for our faults by undergoing a Passion and death which really possess the value of a satisfaction of justice, and this painful satisfaction was willed positively by God as good because making atonement for the sins of mankind; but this divine will does not explain itself, nor ultimately can it be explained save as the overflow of merciful love. In short, retributive justice could not provide the least motive for any part of the satisfaction made by Jesus, even were it for our benefit; yet the fact remains that he redeemed us through the most bitter sufferings. The reason is to be sought in his own and the Father's superabundant mercy.

God might have remitted all satisfaction without injustice

St. Thomas proposes the following objection to himself: If God denied his own justice he would deny himself. But God's justice required that man be redeemed by the satisfaction Christ offered in undergoing his Passion and death. It would seem, therefore, that this satisfaction was necessary and inevitable.

St. Thomas makes the clearing up of this difficulty the occasion for a valuable development. A judge is bound in justice to inflict a penalty when the case concerns a crime against a third party, whether this be a

---

in two vols. by J. Carroll, *The Mystery of Faith*, II (London, 1950), 223.

citizen, the prince, or the community (*rempublicam*). But, should the offence be simply personal to himself then the judge may remit the penalty out of pure mercy without infringing justice. Now God has no superior. He is himself the highest common good of the universe. Hence he may, without injury to anyone, remit the offence of sin without exacting a penalty.[3] God did not, in fact, demand satisfaction under pain of committing an injustice had he failed to do so.

Injustice atoned for by justice

Christ's Passion was the most fitting way we could have been redeemed *(congruentissimus modus)*: man had lost himself by committing an injustice, he would be redeemed by the fulfilment of justice. However, though justice demand that a guilty person should suffer the penalty of his crime, it is not unjust for some friend to come forward and undertake the burden of atoning for the damage and so set him free. Now God alone, because of his infinite dignity, was capable of offering an adequate satisfaction for the sins of all mankind. It was fitting, therefore, that he should suffer for man what man himself had deserved to suffer by his sin.[4]

Materially speaking, everything happens on the cross as though a condemned criminal were paying for his own crimes. Blood is spilt and everything seems to show that Christ's flesh was a sinful flesh. "On the cross, his own body took the weight of our sins; we were to become dead to our sins, and live for holiness" (1 Pet 2:24). God "has set me free, in Jesus Christ, from the principle of sin and of death . . . and this God

---

[3] See IIIa, qu. 46, art. 2, ad 3um.
[4] See *Compendium Theologiae,* cap. 226, n. 470.

has done, by sending us his own Son, *in the fashion* of our guilty nature, to make amends for our guilt. He has signed the death-warrant of sin in our nature, so that we should be fully quit of the law's claim, we, who follow the ways of the spirit, not the ways of flesh and blood" (Rom 8:2–4). This gives us a startling idea of what divine justice could have meant to us, even though the Savior was not condemned by his Father. The torture of Calvary is the most eloquent of warnings against the aberrations of sin. To offend God is to crucify the flesh of Christ all over again. The redemption is a mystery of justice.

A mystery of justice in the strict sense?

Theologians are far from unanimous in answering the question whether Christ made satisfaction for us all with the equivalence required by justice strictly speaking. Some, such as Billot, deny, others, such as Alastruey-Sánchez, affirm that he did so, while yet others, such as Solano, waver between these two opinions.[5] A short analysis of their controversy will furnish us the opportunity to distinguish in what sense redemption may or may not be understood in terms of strict justice.

Catholic doctrine holds that Christ's satisfaction was not only equivalent to, but infinitely exceeded, as such, the offences of the human race.[6] Nevertheless,

---

[5] See Billot, *De Verbo Incarnato* (Rome, 1949), 396–8; Alastruey-Sánchez, *Tractatus de Incarnatione Verbi Dei* (Salamanca, incomplete and undated), 471–82; Solano, *De Verbo Incarnato*, vol. III of *Sacrae Theologiae Summa* in the B.A.C. (Madrid, 1953), 279, n. 665.

[6] In suffering for love and obedience Christ offered God far more than was absolutely necessary to atone for the offences of mankind; first because of the immensity of his charity; secondly because of the life he sacrificed which belonged to one who was God and man; finally because of the extent and depth of his sufferings (IIIa, qu.

maintains Billot, it remains true that Christ could neither merit nor make satisfaction within the full rigor of
justice, since, from this point of view, he is in the same
situation as ourselves. In either case, a strict equivalence has to be excluded. The primary reason Billot
gives for this is that, since justice implies a recipro-
cal obligation (I owe you and you owe me), more is
involved in strictly just compensation than equivalence
between merit and recompense, or between an offence
and its satisfaction. For it is also implied necessarily,
that he who merits or expiates should not be beholden,
as such, to the person whom his acts envisage; that is,
he should owe neither the act itself, nor his ability to
accomplish it to this person. In fact, he must be inde-
pendent. Now our satisfaction for sin, free and meritorious though it is, cannot but be God's gift to us, for
he is the ultimate source of all merit freely consented
to. Hence it is impossible for an act of satisfaction of
this sort to be one which involves strict justice between
ourselves and God—and this holds equally good for
Christ's vicarious satisfaction of his Father. Such is one
aspect, at least, of Billot's thought on the subject.[7]

On the contrary, replies Alastruey-Sánchez, in our
Savior's case, the grace and liberality of the creditor do
not affect the settlement of the debt immediately and
formally, but stand to it as presupposed conditions. The
Incarnation being a gratuitous gift, once it is given,
the Word Incarnate treats with his Father as equal
to equal, and may, therefore, offer satisfaction in the

48, art. 2 corp.).

[7] "It was absolutely impossible for Christ to satisfy or merit in strict
justice" (Billot, *De Verbo Incarnato*, 396). "If there were any question of strict justice Christ as man would have acquired a strict
right with regard to his Father, which is inconceivable" (*ibid.*, 398).

strictest sense of the term.[8]

But both these positions seem to us to need qualification.

We do not think it possible to allow, even implicitly, as Alastruey-Sánchez does, that the mystery of our redemption is a matter of commutative justice between the Father and the Son, as between two equal parties to a contract. The Savior did not redeem us as God, and so as equal to the Father, but as God made man, and after enduring suffering and death in that human nature, according to which he could say: "My Father has greater power than I" (John 14:28). The Word of God is our mediator and high priest inasmuch as he is man. Here, then, we must side unflinchingly with Billot. As man, the Savior has everything from God, including those free and meritorious acts of charity, in virtue of which he redeemed us. From God's point of view, the vicarious satisfaction of Jesus Christ is not an "exchange," achieving equality after the fashion of commutative justice.[9] Our redemption is a gift, that of the Triune God, to the Son of God made man, and, in him, to all the members of his Mystical Body.

But are we, therefore, to conclude that strict justice has *no* bearing on the vicarious satisfaction of our Redeemer? We should not come to such a conclusion

---

[8] "Christ's satisfaction satisfied in strict justice, in the strictest possible sense of the word [*ad strictos iuris apices*]." "Christ's satisfaction is not based on the grace and liberality of the creditor." "Habitual grace and the other supernatural gifts were co-natural to Christ's humanity by reason of the hypostatic union" (Alastruey-Sánchez, *Tractatus de Incarnatione Verbi Dei*, 478, 480). By "co-natural," understand, were *due* to Christ's humanity.

[9] It is proper to Christ as man to be our immediate redeemer, but the first cause of our redemption is the whole of the Blessed Trinity (IIIa, qu. 48, art. 5).

over-hastily, and without the necessary qualifications. For that commutative justice which must always be excluded from the relations existing between a created nature and its Creator is not the only possible type of justice. We should, rather, reconsider the problem in the light of the virtue of religion, which regulates our relations with God, and is included, by way of analogy, in the concept of distributive justice.[10]

From this point of view we can both affirm and deny that our relations with God involve strict justice. This is lacking in so far as we can never adequately either acknowledge the excellence of the Creator's goodness, nor satisfy for the sins which we have committed. But it does enter, and most strictly, in our duty to adore God and to satisfy for our sins. The very transcendence of God is the reason why such obligations are disproportionate to the demands they make. "Man owes God whatsoever he renders to him, but he never achieves equivalence; he can never render as much as he owes."[11]

The subsequent question, as to whether we must make the full satisfaction for our sins required by strict justice, has to be answered without prejudice to this mystery of our relations with God. We can safeguard it here by means of an important distinction between our *duty* to satisfy strictly for our sins, which is always with us, and our *ability* to make such satisfaction adequately, which is always lacking to us. Put briefly and schematically, it may be said that we *must* do all that

---

[10] Inasmuch as we give God that which we *owe* him whenever we acknowledge his sovereignty as Creator. See IIa IIae, qu. 81 and qu. 61, art. 1, ad 3um.

[11] IIa IIae, qu. 80, art. 1 and qu. 81. This is yet another aspect of the mystery of the creature's relationship to his infinite Creator.

we *can*, but on the other hand, we *cannot* do all that we *ought*.

In the case of our Savior the roles are reversed. Where we *ought* and *cannot*, he *can* but *need* not. For Jesus is not bound to anything in strict justice (the aspect of duty). On the other hand, any satisfaction he does offer for us will be not only adequate to, but greatly in excess of, even the most rigorous possible requirements of strict justice (the aspect of capability).

Christ could take on neither our sin, nor, love apart, the personal obligation to satisfy justice for this sin. Yet, out of love, he did will with entire liberty to take on himself this satisfaction of justice through his obedience to the commands of his Father. In so doing, he acknowledged and respected the strictest rights of divine justice—not in relation to himself but to us—just as, by the same token, he acknowledged and respected, not his duty, but ours, in face of this same justice. Those sufferings, which were satisfaction for sin, were undertaken in our name and for our benefit. The Son of God lovingly sacrificed himself for us wretched sinners. Although not in any way obliged, he was both able and willing to do so.

Once he had made this satisfaction it could not but be superabundant.[12] If he who does more than he must accomplishes thereby all that duty requires, what

---

[12] Reflection will show that an adequate satisfaction—in the mathematical sense—for sin as an offence against God is inconceivable and unobtainable. Only where God had offended God could God repair his offence in a way that would be neither deficient nor superabundant; but the hypothesis is absurd and blasphemous: the Savior neither sinned nor assumed our sin. On the other hand, the satisfaction of man, a pure creature, must always be inadequate because of God's infinite transcendence.

is to be said of him who, while bound to nothing, yet exceeds all the possible requirements of duty? Our Savior's atonement was not merely strictly adequate but in excess of strict sufficiency and overwhelmingly abundant.[13] Here there is no suspicion of a strictness which takes the form of vengeance upon sinners. The divine justice, revealed in the Person of God's Son, the Holy One *par excellence*, overwhelms our categories. Having said that it is God who makes atonement for man we have said all.

Whether one meditates on the mystery of strict justice in relation to this vicarious satisfaction from the point of view of *duty* or of *ability* to satisfy, in the sense in which we have defined those terms, one cannot but find love. Christ was under no obligation to suffer in order to atone for our sins: love alone could move him to it, and once he did so, he left strict requirements behind. The justice of Calvary can only be explained by love. It is, and can only be, justice in love. And here we have reached the deepest aspect of the mystery.[14]

---

[13] This is the teaching of the *Catechism of the Council of Trent*: "Though God should wish to demand satisfaction to the fullest extent of his right [*summo iure*] all has been more than fully settled [*cumulate, plenissime*] by Christ, our Lord" (Pars IIa, cap. 5. n. 62–3).

[14] To sum up: the acts of the Son of God made man have an infinite value because of the Person acting but not because of the human nature in which he acts: the Word Incarnate is equal with his Father in so far as he is the Word, but inferior and submitted to him in the work of his redemptive Incarnation. This is the balance to be maintained in the mystery of the hypostatic union. Because Jesus is God, his vicarious satisfaction has infinitely superabundant value; because Jesus saves us as man, this satisfaction is a *gift* of God and is due to God's grace and liberality. The vicarious satisfaction can be linked to distributive justice in so far as the Savior lovingly desired to satisfy *in our place* and for our benefit (which he did superabundantly), which makes his act one of loving justice.

WHAT IS REDEMPTION?

Through the superabundance of God's mercy

Let us try to see in the mystery of our redemption "both the *severity* of God, who did not wish to remit sin without satisfaction, for which reason the Apostle says: 'He did not even spare his own Son,' and his *goodness*, since, when man was unable to make adequate satisfaction, whatever the penalty he suffered, God gave him a liberator *(satis-factorem)*, and, as the Apostle also says, 'gave him up for us all'; for 'God has offered him to us as a means of reconciliation, in virtue of faith, ransoming us with his blood' (Rom 3:25)".[15]

> That mankind should be liberated through the Passion of Christ was in keeping with both God's mercy and his justice. With his justice, because Christ, by his Passion, made satisfaction for the sin of the human race and so man is liberated by Christ's justice; with his mercy, because when man could not satisfy by himself for the sin of all human kind, God gave him his own Son to be his liberator. And in this *God showed greater mercy than if he had forgiven sin without demanding satisfaction*; and so we read in the Epistle to the Ephesians: "How

---

Mgr. Journet, following John of St. Thomas, expresses this very well: "Herein lies the mystery of the redemption: it is the paradox of a mercy which is owed, and of a justice which is gratuitous. For redemption is an act of mercy to men but one which is owing to Christ and could not be refused him without injustice. It is, therefore, an act of justice in Christ's regard but by no means owing to men, who have nothing to give in exchange for their sins; nothing, that is, apart from Christ who spontaneously gives himself to them to be good for everything" (*L'Eglise du Verbe Incarne*, II, Paris, 1951, 208). God *owes it to himself* (*sibi debet*, Ia, qu. 25, art. 5, ad 2um, and qu. 21, art. 1) to accept the offering of our Redeemer.

[15] IIIa, qu. 47, art. 3, ad 1um.

rich is God in mercy, with what an excess of love he loved us! Our sins had made dead men of us, and he, in giving life to Christ, gave life to us too" (2:4–5).[16]

The words we have emphasized seem to us to express with a maximum of depth, simplicity and clarity the dominant intuition of St. Thomas in this treatise of the redemption. The redeeming love shows at one and the same time two complementary moral truths, the one, the gravity of our sin, being the occasion of the other, the divine mercy. Sin is nothing else but hatred of God, hatred of Love, the doing to death of God in the soul. Yet, by the same token that he moves us to horror of sin, God shows himself just and merciful. For could he have chosen any better way to bring home the malice of sin to us than in allowing it to be the occasion of Christ's death on the cross?

Here, also, we may see how atonement for sin manifested a divine love beyond our wildest dreams to imagine; for there is no greater mercy than to give one's life-blood for one's enemies, and God has died for us sinners. As the liturgy of the Easter vigil makes so bold as to sing: "Happy the fault that merited such a redeemer!"

God's wishes and permissions are the answer to everything. We can only adore him.

Historically, it is through sin that death entered the world, and the unreality of liberal theology becomes all too apparent when it relegates Christ's Passion to being merely and exclusively an example of heroic courage and a token of love. How could it have been appropri-

---

[16] IIIa, qu. 46, art. 1, ad 3um.

ate for the Son of God to suffer a bloody death if he had not wished to atone for sin? Only atonement for sin can explain the cross. Without this justice (the debt of reparation for sin) we should never have known this mercy (which paid the debt); but, on the other hand, failing this mercy we should never have known the justice which is fulfilled; for it is mercy which dominates and is triumphant while justice is fulfilled in the atonement apart from and in excess of its own requirements.

Apart from: for justice can do nothing to the innocent.

In excess of: because "the least suffering of Christ would have been enough to redeem all the sins of the human race."[17] As love grows, so the need for suffering disappears, and our Savior's love was infinitely valuable. Jesus could, therefore, have redeemed us without suffering at all.

Although we can and must believe that divine justice is revealed on the cross in the crucified flesh of Christ, which is the flesh of a victim offered in a sacrifice of expiation (Rom 3:24–26), it is also urgent to state clearly that the Word in his sacred flesh could only be the victim of his own merciful love. His is a loving atonement. Mercy, and mercy alone, proposes, penetrates and decides upon the sacrifice of Calvary. Indeed, it is only by and through mercy that this sacrifice becomes a possibility. And thus the redemption becomes for him who can read the visible and sanguinary expression of the priority which divine love has over the order of justice at the mysterious point of their union in God. Justice in God is not separable from love but is, on the contrary, aflame with love. It is there,

---

[17] *Ibid.*, art. 5, ad 3um.

above all, one and the same thing as love itself.

Here we touch on the mystery of the divine attributes which entail each other mutually in virtue of God's ineffable transcendence. God uses this gesture of surpassing love to reveal himself and by himself something of his justice. This justice cannot appear in the Person of the Son of God otherwise than in the form of love. Yet love in God is not distinct from justice, and it is this love which is the object of the mystery of the redemption. That is why this mystery infinitely exceeds our grasp and we fail to understand it. Whichever way we look at it, mercy first and then justice, or justice and then mercy, we find the same, that God desired mercy in justice and justice in mercy. Both are revealed together and inseparably though mercy remains preeminent. They are expressions of the love of God who frees us from sin in drawing us to himself. God is love.

The wounded heart of our Savior reveals the love which achieves our salvation. We have to learn how to relate spontaneously the blood of this heart to the impetus of love which inflames Christ's human will, and to relate this impetus itself to the respiration of love which marks the rhythm of life in the Trinity. Jesus, conceived of the Holy Spirit in the womb of the Virgin Mary, whose own heart was spotless, lives and dies for love. His heart keeps the stigmata of suffering after his victorious Resurrection because they are the living symbols of those bonds of merciful love, which, in the Mystical Body, bind Head to members in the unity of the Holy Spirit.[18]

---

[18] See Philippe de la Trinité, "Du Coeur du Christ a l'esprit d'amour," in *Etudes Carmelitaines*, 1950, 387.

THE SUFFERINGS OF THE PASSION

There is no theological romanticism in St. Thomas' analysis of Christ's sufferings during the Passion. For him, there is no positive abandonment, no antagonism, no wrath on the side of the Father; no infernal punishments on that of the Son. St. Thomas even refuses to compare our Savior's sufferings with the eventual expiation and purification which souls in purgatory will undergo after their death.[19] This is understandable, for Christ is God and innocence itself.

Moreover, St. Thomas notices that Jesus did not say: "I am sorrowful," but: "*My soul* is sorrowful even unto death," because "I" expresses the person, and Christ was not sorrowful in so far as he was the Word of God, but only in the human soul he had assumed into the unity of his person.[20] God as God does not suffer but he did suffer inasmuch as he was man. Of Jesus it must be said: "That man is God and has suffered."

The physical, psychological, and moral sufferings

St. Thomas makes a striking summary of Christ's sufferings in order to emphasize their universality, not in the absolute sense of the word (Christ could not, for example, have been the victim of fire and water at the same time) but in a sense sufficiently true to justify, as he explains, its use here.

Who made him suffer? All made him suffer: Jews and Gentiles, men and women (the maids accusing

---

[19] See IIIa, qu. 46, art. 6, ad 3um.

[20] See *Comm. in Matt.* 26, n. 2224. St. Thomas seems unaware that the semitism, "my soul is sorrowful" stands for, "I am sorrowful," but his theological exegesis remains exact.

Peter), important people and servants, anonymous people, friends and acquaintances (Judas betrays him, Peter denies him). In what did he suffer? In his friends who abandoned him, in his reputation (the blasphemies), in his honour and his glory (the insults and mockeries), in the property he owned (he is stripped of his garments), in his soul (sorrow, disgust, fear) and in his body (the sores and wounds). As regards this last point he was spared nothing.

For Jesus suffered in his head (the spittle, the cuffs, the crown of sharp thorns), in his hands and feet (pierced by nails) and from the scourging as well as from many other indignities. None of the five senses was spared: neither touch (the nails and lashes), nor taste (the vinegar and aloes), nor smell (the fetid stench of the corpses left on Calvary), nor hearing (the blasphemies and insults), nor sight (he saw the anguish of his mother and the disciple he loved).[21]

After he has recalled such sufferings, St. Thomas goes on to ask himself whether they were not deeper than any which man may suffer in this life. He answers affirmatively on account of both the physical pain and the interior sorrow, and supports his conclusion by repeating or completing what he has just said.

To consider, first of all, the cause of those sufferings: death by crucifixion is one of the most excruciating because the victim is fastened to the wood by nails driven into the most sensitive joints and his torment is increased by the weight of his body as well as by the length of time he must suffer. It is not the sudden death of a sword-stroke. Christ's interior suf-

---

[21] See IIIa, qu. 46, art. 5. The suffering attributed to the sense of smell lacks historical foundation.

fering, on the other hand, was due primarily to all the sins of mankind for which he offered satisfaction in his torments. These sins he ascribes to himself, saying with the Psalmist, "The words of my sins" (Ps 21:2, Douay). The sorrow of Jesus for the sins of humanity immeasurably surpassed that which a particular sinner might feel for his own offences, and this both because it proceeded from a greater wisdom and charity and because it extended to all the sins of the world. But in Jesus this was not a sorrow of contrition for he was, and knew that he was, innocent.[22]

Among the sins from which Christ suffered there stand out especially that of the Jews and those who were accessories to the crime of his death, above all, also, the fault of the disciples who took scandal during the course of the Passion.

The more sensitive one is the more one suffers. But Christ was possessed of the finest sensibility. His body had been miraculously fashioned by the Holy Spirit. His soul could not have felt the causes of its suffering more acutely. "It is not as if our high priest was incapable of feeling for us in our humiliations; he has been through every trial, fashioned as we are, only sinless" (Heb 4:15).

What purity there was in this suffering and sorrow! Christ did not wish to seek or accept the least

---

[22] To the objection that Christ's knowledge of his own innocence must have contributed to relieve his sufferings since his own guilt could not have afflicted him, St. Thomas replies: it is true that Christ did not suffer from any guilt of his own. but the better an innocent man knows how undeserved are his sufferings the more affliction they cause him (IIIa, qu. 46, art. 6, ad 5um). Nevertheless (see above), the suffering of the innocent man is lightened to the extent that he suffers for love.

relief in the midst of his torments because he had assumed them voluntarily in order to set us free. Since he desired to make a just satisfaction, not only did he consider the infinite value of the least pain suffered by God and man but he bore such suffering as might appropriately be borne in order to make satisfaction by the nature which he had assumed.[23]

In peace and joyfulness

Christ's deepest natural will senses the horror of death, but, in his deliberate will, under the control of his surpassing love, he generously wishes to die.[24] The sweat of blood in the garden of Olives does not lessen his acceptance: "Father, all things are possible to thee; take away this chalice from before me; only as thy will is, not as mine is" (Mark 14:36). On the other hand, such a loving submission could not but sweeten the Passion of Christ.

> We read in St. John: "And now my soul is distressed. What am I to say? I will say, Father, save me from undergoing this hour of trial; and yet I have only reached this hour of trial that I might undergo it" (John 12:27).
>
> It is to be noted that this is not a spontaneous request of Christ's reason but that this reason becomes here the advocate, as it were, and the mouthpiece of his sensitive nature which was loath to die. This is the reaction which his reason here

---

[23] We translate the *sufficeret* of St. Thomas as "might appropriately be borne" because of the context. But this suffering of satisfaction is not in fact considered in abstraction from the hypostatic union, apart from which no suffering could have sufficed in justice.

[24] See IIIa, qu. 18, art. 5 and art. 6.

manifests. Hence we can solve the problem raised by the text: "Christ offered prayer . . . with such piety as won him a hearing" (Heb 5:7), which does not seem to be borne out here. We say, therefore, that Christ was heard on every occasion when it was his earnest intention that he should be heard. Here, by asking a rhetorical question, he shows the nature of his feelings. For, as St. John Chrysostom remarked, the expression should be taken negatively, the sense being: And what am I to say? shall I say: Father, save me from this hour of trial? By which he means: No, I shall not say that.[25]

Divine providence is not to be resisted, for, as Job says: "Who hath resisted him, and hath had peace?" (9:4, Douay). The Passion is to be a cup (in the original text) because it has a sweetness from the charity of the sufferer though of itself it contains only bitterness. Just as, for example, a healing medicine may be sweetened by the hope of regaining one's health, however bitter its taste. "I will take the cup that is pledge of my deliverance, and invoke the name of the Lord upon it" (Ps 115:13). This cup was given Christ by the Father in so far as he freely accepted the Passion in conformity with the Father's will.[26]

We should observe that, if Christ drained his cup at one draught, the members of his Mystical Body, apostles and saints, sipped, as it were, at theirs, in so far as they drank of the cup with repugnance; because even in the fine point of their will they did not accept it so well as he. For this

---

[25] See *Comm. in Joan.* 12, lect. 5, n. 1658.
[26] See *Ibid.*, 18, lect. 2, n. 2293.

very reason Christ had in a sense less to suffer.[27]

Everything is easy, O God, for him whom you love, save only not to accomplish your adorable will.[28]

But more is to come. For the Savior, even in his moments of greatest agony, never ceased to enjoy the beatific vision. This is St. Thomas' teaching and common doctrine in theology. The mystery involved is squarely faced by St. Thomas who seeks neither to minimize it nor to explain it away. He expresses it as best he can.

Examples may help us to symbolize this mystery. For instance, the summit of a mountain may be scorched by the sun while the plains below remain shrouded in mist; or we have the spectacle of the martyrs who kept their joy and peace even when their bodies were being racked with torture. But Christ's case is unique and no limits can be set to it.

We must not say that Christ suffered in his body but not in his soul. The dichotomy would be artificial, for man must be taken as a whole. Besides, Scripture is perfectly clear: "My soul," Jesus says, "is sorrowful even unto death." Christ suffered as men suffer, for physical, psychological and moral reasons. Nevertheless, the Son of God always possessed at the highest point of his human intelligence and will both the vision of himself and the Father and the peace and unutterable joy which flow from that vision. At a lower level Christ's intellect and will shrank from suffering and death, but on the higher level no anguish, struggle or difficulties

---

[27] See *Comm. in Cant.* Cant., alt. exp., 7, 658.
[28] See Paul Claudel, *L'Otage, ibid.*

could exist for him; all was dissolved by the gentle and calming light of an infinitely wise love.

The lucid and penetrating gaze of St. Thomas does not shrink from approaching the most tragic depths of sadness in Christ's heart because of his love (for his offended Father and for those who offend him) in the face of the sins of the world (hating sin but respecting the liberty of sinners). St. Thomas may cause us surprise, but on reflection he satisfies. We should learn to confront, steadily and without false sentimentalism, the issue of our last end. It is the truth alone which will set us free.

It is natural that one should suffer from the evils threatening those dear to one, and here again Christ was greatly saddened by men's sins and the punishments due to them. But his sadness was not like ours since, in so far as he enjoyed the beatific vision, Christ saw everything from the higher vantage point of divine Wisdom and could not, therefore, from this point of view, be saddened by anything—whether by sin or by the punishment it entails for sinners. This is the state of the blessed in heaven who refer everything to the dispositions of divine Wisdom. Our case is different because we may sometimes think that the salvation of certain souls would contribute to God's honor and to the exaltation of the faith, and are saddened by their sins; they will be damned in fact but we are unaware of this.

Christ could rejoice at the apex of his spirit in what he suffered in his senses, his imagination and his lower reason; for this is the mystery of simultaneous joy and pain which, while they differ in origin, co-exist in a single subject. At the highest point nothing could have caused him sadness, but on a lower level he was immersed in suffering. For in his case joy did not lessen suffering nor did suffering hinder joy. Neither of these states of mind affected the other.[29]

God's joy is infinite.[30] Jesus as man never failed to share in this joy through the beatific vision, and it was to this joy that he came to invite us at the cost of his sufferings.

Take, for example, these words from his discourse to the Apostles after the Last Supper and before his agony in the garden: "I have bestowed my love upon you just as my Father has bestowed his love upon me; live on, then, in my love. You will live on in my love, if you keep my commandments, just as it is by keeping my Father's commandments that I live on in his love. All this I have told you, so that my joy may be yours, and the measure of your joy may be filled up. This is my commandment, that you should love one another, as I have loved you. This is the greatest love a man can show, that he should lay down his life for his friends" (John 15:9–13). Let us enter into the joy of God, our master, even at the price of the cross (Matt 25:23).

SOME CASES OF DIFFICULT EXEGESIS

There are some texts from Scripture which have been interpreted in a way impossible to reconcile with St. Thomas' theological teaching on the redemption. Sometimes this is due to over-hasty and superficial reading. At all events, we should remember both that the letter kills while it is the spirit which gives life and that texts must always be considered in their imme-

---

[29] See *Compendium Theologiae,* cap. 232, n. 492 and n. 494.
[30] See IIa IIae, qu. 28, art. 3 corp.

diate or remote context. We shall follow St. Thomas'
exegesis of these difficult texts. He may occasionally
express himself clumsily or repetitively but his coher-
ence and fidelity to the sacred authors should be more
than enough to reassure us.

The suffering Servant

"Here is one despised, left out of all human reckoning
. . . . Our weakness, it was he who carried the weight
of it, our miseries, and it was he who bore them . . .
and all the while it was for our sins he was wounded,
it was guilt of ours crushed him down. . . . It is for my
people's sake I have smitten him. . . . Ay, the Lord's
will it was, overwhelmed he should be with trouble"
(Isa 53:3–5, 8, 10). St. Thomas comments:

> Christ, during his Passion, being true man of flesh
> and bone, bore our weaknesses such as hunger and
> thirst, and the sufferings of our sensitive nature,
> such as sadness. He rid us of sin and underwent
> its penalties in our place. He was wounded by the
> thorns, the nails and the lance; he was bruised by
> the blows and beatings, in order to obliterate our
> sins. He bore for us the punishments due to our
> sins, and, thanks to his peace-making, we have
> access to God. He offered himself to God as a vic-
> tim for our salvation. He was the most despised of
> men because of the harshness of his suffering, the
> shame of his death and the enormity of the crime
> attributed to him; he was the man of sorrows. His
> Father accepted his Passion: "for the wickedness
> of my people have I struck him," that is, have I

allowed him to be struck.[31] He was obedient to his Father to death itself, and thus achieved the justification of mankind.[32]

The abandonment

"And about the ninth hour, Jesus cried out with a loud voice, Eli, Eli, lamma sabachthani? that is, My God, my God, why hast thou forsaken me?" (Matt 27:46). St. Thomas comments:

> These words are taken from psalm twenty-one which seems to refer especially to Christ's Passion. What is their meaning here, as spoken by him?
>
> Someone may be said to have been forsaken by God when God does not show him his presence in protecting him and listening to his petitions. And so Christ, in so far as he was not spared his bodily sufferings, was forsaken for a time by his Father. "He did not even spare his own Son" (Rom 8:32).
>
> The psalm continues: "Far from my salvation are the words of my sins" (Douay Version for the Vulgate's *verba delictorum meorum*), and they show that I am not just but a sinner. These words are not applied personally to Christ but only in the name of sinners or of the Church. For we normally find, when we interpret the psalms, that Christ applies to himself what is appropriate to his members, insofar as Christ and the Church are the one Mystical Body. Christ transforms himself into the

---

[31] St. Thomas quotes the Latin text: *Propter scelus populi mei percussi eum.* Mgr. Knox's version, made in the light of the Hebrew original, bears out St. Thomas' exegesis: "Be sure it is for my people's sake I have smitten him."

[32] *Comm. in Isaiam*, 53, XIX, 32–4 *passim.*

Church and the Church is transformed into Christ. But though it be true that there are sins in Christ's members, that is, in the Church, it is not true that there are any in the head, that is, in Christ himself: Christ on the cross had only the outward appearance of a sinner. "God has done (what the law could not do) by sending us his own Son, in the fashion of our sinful nature, to make amends for our guilt" (Rom 8:3). "Christ never knew sin, and God made him into sin for us, so that in him we might be turned into the holiness of God" (2 Cor 5:21).[33]

Christ speaks as man: he repeats, "My God, my God," to manifest the depth of his feelings. He uses the word "forsaken" metaphorically *(per similitudinem)* because, since all that we have comes from God, when a person is left to fall into the evil of punishment for sin, he is said to be forsaken by God. Christ was abandoned not as regards the hypostatic union, nor as regards grace, but in relation to the Passion. He says, "Why," not to express reluctance but in compassion for the Jews in their darkness . . . and in his wonder at his Father's love of sinners.[34]

---

[33] *Comm. in Pss.* 21, n. 1, 344.

[34] *Comm. in Matt.* 27, n. 2383. The words of Mgr. Journet are of interest: "Jesus did not fear for the salvation of his soul. He did not think that God was punishing him; he did not suffer the torments of the damned. He did suffer both morally and physically beyond anything of which we have experience on this earth. He could see each one of our sins, each of my betrayals, each of my denials of his truth. Above all, he saw that horrifying contempt with which souls try to cut themselves off from his love. His is the suffering of the Savior of the world, not that of one who is damned; it is satisfaction not punishment. It is not despairing but full of light.

But the luminous suffering of a God who dies for us is more heartrending than the suffering of despair. To this suffering alone is it given to plumb the depths of the abyss which separates good

To show his justice

"God has offered him (Jesus Christ) to us as a means of reconciliation, in virtue of faith, ransoming us with his blood. Thus God has vindicated his own holiness, showing us why he overlooked our former sins in the days of his forbearance; and he has also vindicated the holiness of Jesus Christ, here and now, as one who is himself holy, and imparts holiness to those who take their stand upon faith in him" (Rom 3:25–26).

St. Thomas does not mention retributive justice once in the long commentary which he devotes to these verses. According to him, they speak of the efficacy of Christ's blood for the remission of our sins, and it is

---

from evil, heaven from hell, love from hate, the 'Yes' addressed to God from the 'No.' This suffering alone may know exhaustively, assume in its entirety and offer to God the price asked for redemption from evil and for the reformation of the world." *Les Sept Paroles du Christ au Croix* (Paris, 1954), 88–90.

The exegesis of Christ's abandonment on the Cross has taken various permissible forms. St. John of the Cross, for example, writes: "It is certain that, at the moment of his (Christ's) death, he was likewise annihilated in his soul, and was deprived of any relief and consolation, since his Father left him in the most intense *aridity* according to the lower part of his nature...This was the greatest desolation with respect *to sense* that he had suffered in his life...," and he was most completely annihilated with respect to his Father "since at that time he forsook him that he might pay the whole of man's debt and unite him with God, being thus annihilated and reduced, as it were, to nothing." *Subida del Monte Carmelo*, lib. 2, cap. 7. English translation of E. Allison Peers, *Complete Works of St. John of the Cross*, I, 92. The emphasis is ours. St. John seems to be speaking here of an abandonment by God on the sensitive level, that at which St. Thomas easily admits that anguish and sorrow could have caused the sweat of blood. Supposing this to be the case, the Mystical Doctor would have introduced an element of suffering unknown to the Angelic Doctor, yet without speaking of wrath or anger on God's part, and still less of the suffering of damnation.

this which shows us God's justice (i.e. holiness), both that by which he himself is just and that by which he justifies others.

> The Apostle speaks here of the vindication of God's holiness. First of all he deals with the manner of this vindication, saying: "In order to vindicate his holiness," as though he were to say, this was done in order that we might be sanctified by Christ's redemption through faith in his blood, since the forgiveness of our former sins itself shows forth God's holiness. For God shows how necessary his own holiness is for man in remitting the sins committed under the old law, against which man was powerless to guard himself but which the old law itself could not forgive him. Only through faith in Christ's blood can sins, whether past or present, be forgiven; but those who lived before Christ's Passion could have the faith which we have now and which ensures the efficacy of that Passion . . . "and we too speak our minds with full confidence, sharing that same faith" (2 Cor 4:13).
>
> When the Apostle comes to the time of that vindication he adds: "Showing us why he overlooked our former sins in the days of his forbearance" as much as to say, the sins previous to Christ's Passion were committed at a time when God seemed to be waiting; for those who committed them, and yet had faith and repented, were not simply condemned nor yet wholly absolved in order to enter immediately into eternal glory. . . . Alternatively, we may say that the holy Fathers of the Old Testament were waiting for God *(in sustentatione Dei)* because they were detained in limbo, not suffering any sensible

pain but waiting to enter into glory through the Passion of Christ. . . .

Finally the Apostle shows how God's holiness is made manifest by the remission of sins, whether this holiness be understood as that whereby God is holy or as that whereby he sanctifies others. And he adds: "As one who is himself holy" as much as to say, God himself appears holy through the remission of sins both because he forgives them as he had promised and because it is appropriate for God to destroy sin by leading men back to himself: "The Lord is just, and just are the deeds he loves" (Ps 10:8).[35]

In the fashion of our guilty nature

"There was something the law could not do—and this God has done, by sending us his own Son, in the fashion of our guilty nature, to make amends for our guilt" (Rom 8:3).

This text does not mean that Christ had merely the likeness or appearance of flesh, as the Manichees claimed, for our Lord himself says: "A spirit has not flesh and bones, as you see that I have" (Luke 24:39), and St. Paul does not write "in the fashion of nature" but, "in the fashion of our guilty nature." Our Lord did not possess a sinful flesh, that is, conceived with sin; for his flesh was conceived by the Holy Spirit who takes away sin: "It is by the power of the Holy Ghost that she has conceived this child" (Matt 1:20). "But, as for me, I have

---

[35] *Comm. in Rom.* 3, lect. 3, n. 310–12. See Lyonnet, in *Introduction a la Bible,* II, 852, 856, 857.

walked in my innocence" (Ps 25:11, Douay). But Christ had the fashion of guilty flesh, that is, flesh resembling sinful flesh, insofar as he could suffer, since man's flesh was not liable to suffering before sin: "And so he must needs become altogether like his brethren . . . to make atonement for the sins of the people" (Heb 2:17).[36]

These commentaries make no mention of an accursed flesh taking our place and substituting for us in face of the divine revenge. The interpretation is simple: flesh which can suffer is said to be "in the fashion of guilty flesh" because suffering entered the world only as a consequence of sin.

The decree of condemnation nailed to the cross

"And in giving life to him, he gave life to you too, when you lay dead in your sins . . . he condoned all your sins, cancelled the deed which excluded us, the decree made to our prejudice, swept it out of the way, by nailing it to the cross" (Col 2:13–14).

> When a person had fully honored his debts it was customary to destroy the documentary evidence of his obligation. But man was living in sin and Christ paid for his freedom with suffering; hence the Apostle's expression. . . . In making satisfaction to God on the cross, he took the consequences of our sin.[37]

---

[36] *Comm. in Rom.* 8, lect. 1, n. 608. See *Comm. in Hebr.* 2, lect. 4, n. 139, and *Comm. in Col.* 2, lect. 3, n. 105.

[37] *Comm. in Col.* 2, lect. 3, n. 115.

God made him into sin for us

"Christ never knew sin, and God made him into sin for us, so that in him we might be turned into the holiness of God" (2 Cor 5:21).

> "God made him into sin for us." This may be interpreted in three ways. Firstly, in view of the fact that under the old law a sin-offering was called "sin": "They (the priests) shall eat the sins of my people and shall lift up their souls to their iniquity" (Hos 4:8, Douay), that is, they shall eat the sin-offerings. And thus the sense of "he was made into sin" is that he was made a victim or sacrifice for sin. Secondly, inasmuch as "sin" may stand for resemblance to sin or punishment for sin, as, for example, in: "God sent us his Son, in the fashion of our guilty nature, to make amends for our guilt" (Rom 8:3); in which case what is meant is that God made him assume a mortal body capable of suffering. Thirdly, inasmuch as something is said to be this or that, not because it really is so, but because it is thought to be so. The meaning would then be that God made Christ pass for a sinner: "He would be counted among the wrongdoers" (Isa 53:12).[38]

Penal substitution is not referred to in these texts, still less is it brought in to make vicarious satisfaction seem more plausible in terms of retributive justice.

Christ himself becoming an accursed thing

"From this curse invoked by the law Christ has ransomed us, by himself becoming, for our sakes, an

---

[38] *Comm. in 2 Cor.* 5, lect. 5, n. 201.

accursed thing; we read that, There is a curse on the man who hangs on a gibbet" (Gal 3:13).

When the Apostle says: "becoming, for our sakes, an accursed thing," he explains how we were set free. Now an accursed thing is an evil thing, and, just as there are two kinds of evil, namely the evil of sin and the evil of punishment, so there are two kinds of curse and, consequently, two different ways of interpreting this passage.

Christ, then, redeemed us from the evil of *sin*—taking our text in the first sense—and this he did by becoming himself an accursed thing, just as he redeemed us from death by dying. Not that there was any sin in him: "He did no wrong, no treachery was found on his lips" (1 Pet 2:22), but he was accursed in the opinion of others, chiefly the Jews, who thought him a sinner. "We would not have given him up to thee, if he had not been a malefactor" (John 18:30). "Christ never knew sin, and God made him into sin for us" (2 Cor 5:21). The Apostle is careful to say "an accursed thing" and not simply "accursed" (*maledictus*) in order to show that the Jews held him to be consummate wickedness *(sceleratissimum)*. "This man can be no messenger from God; he does not observe the sabbath" (John 9:16). "It is not for any deed of mercy we are stoning thee; it is for blasphemy; it is because thou, who art a man, dost pretend to be God" (John 10:33). . . .

Taking the same text in the sense of the evil of *punishment*, then, Christ freed us from our punishment in suffering it himself, death included. But this punishment was ours due to the curse of sin. Therefore, when he died for us, he took this curse of sin upon himself and is said to have become an accursed thing for us. Which is similar to what is said in the Epistle to the Romans: "God sent his Son, in the fashion of our guilty nature," that is, in mortal flesh; and, "Christ never knew sin and God made him into sin for us," that is, he suffered the punishment of sin when he offered himself for our sins.[39]

In short, then, Christ is Innocence itself and has offered himself for our sins. He has redeemed us by himself becoming the priest and victim of a sacrifice of atonement. He was never the object of God's curse.

"He did not even spare his own Son but gave him up for us" (Rom 8:32)

> When he says that the Father did not even spare . . . this means "did not absolve from suffering"—for he had no sin from which to be absolved. It would be irrelevant to quote here: "Spare the rod, and thou art no friend to thy son" (Prov 13:24). But it was not for the sake of his Son—for he is in all things perfect God—that God failed to spare him and subjected him to suffering, but for our sakes. And so St. Paul says: "He gave him up for us all," that is, he exposed him to the Passion for the atonement of our sins; and elsewhere, he describes Christ as "handed over to death for our sins" (Rom 4:25). "God laid on his shoulders our guilt, the guilt of us all" (Isa 53:6).
> The Father handed him over to death in decree-

---

[39] *Comm. in Gal.* 3, lect. 5, n. 148–9. See *ibid.*, n. 150, and *Comm. in Pss.* 40, n. 7, 484.

ing his Incarnation and suffering, and in inspiring
in his human will the love of charity which would
lead him spontaneously to accept his Passion. Thus
Christ is also said to have handed himself over: "He
gave himself up on our behalf" (Eph 5:2).

Everything is to be found in the Son of God as
in its first and precontaining cause *(sicut in primor-
diali et praeoperativa causa):* "He takes precedency
of all, and in him all subsist" (Col 1:17). Hence,
if he is given us everything is given us; as St. Paul
continues: "and must not that gift"—the Son given
us by the Father—"be accompanied by the gift of all
else?"—that is, the gift of all that can work to our
advantage: on the highest level, the divine Person,
given us for our enjoyment; then the intellectual
spirits, given to us for our company; and finally, the
lower creation, given us for our utility in both bad
times and good. "Everything is for you . . . and you
for Christ, and Christ for God" (1 Cor 3:21–22).
And thus it is evident that "those who fear him
never go wanting" (Ps 33:10).[40]

---

[40] *Comm. in Rom.* 8, lect. 6, n. 713–14. The theological outlook of
some of the commentaries of the Jerusalem Bible upon St. Paul is
not always that of St. Thomas. E.g., commenting Col. 2:14: "The
old law, in forbidding sin, only had the effect of condemning the
man who transgressed it to death (cf. Rom. 7:7) . . . God quashed
this condemnation when he executed it upon the person of his Son
after having 'made him into sin' (2 Cor. 5:21), 'a subject of the law'
(Gal. 4:4), and 'cursed' by it (Gal. 3:13). He gave him up to death
on the Cross, nailing to the wood and cancelling the deed which
recorded our debt and condemned us."

Commenting 2 Cor. 5:21: "Juridically God has identified Jesus
with sin and brought down on him the curse incurred by sin (Gal.
3:13; Rom. 8:3)".

And Gal. 3:13: "Christ, in order to free men from the divine curse
which violation of the law had brought down upon them, came and

Christ the Redeemer is the gift *par excellence* of the Father, the most sublime evidence of his love for us.

The theology of the Doctor of the *Summa Theologica* is echoed by that of the Doctor of the *Living Flame of Love*, as this beautiful "Prayer of the Enamored Soul" bears witness.

> O Lord, my Love, if thou art still mindful of my sins, and wilt not grant my petitions, thy will be done, for that is my chief desire. Show thou thy goodness and mercy and thou shalt be known by them. If it be that thou art waiting for my good works, that in them thou mayest grant my petition, do thou give them and work in me: send also the penalties which thou wilt accept, and do thou inflict them. But if thou art not waiting for my good works, what art thou waiting for, O most merciful Lord? Why tarriest thou? For if at last it must be grace and mercy, for which I pray in thy Son, do thou accept my worthless offering, according to thy holy will, and give me this good since thou also dost desire it.
>
> Who can free himself from base and mean ways, if thou, O my God, wilt not lift him up to thee in pure love? How shall a man raise himself up to thee, being born and bred in misery, if thou wilt not lift him up with the hand that made him? Thou

---

shared it himself . . . The undoubtedly remote analogy of Christ crucified and the man accursed of Deuteronomy 21:13, is only an illustration of this doctrine."

On the other hand, we read for Matt. 27:46 (*ut quid dereliquisti me*): "This is a cry of real distress but not of despair: this complaint, borrowed from Scripture, is a prayer to God which is followed in the psalm by joyful assurance of the ultimate triumph."

wilt not take away from me, O my God, what thou hast once given me in thy only-begotten Son, Jesus Christ, in whom thou hast given me all I desire. I will therefore rejoice; thou wilt not tarry if I wait for thee. Why art thou waiting then, O my soul, since even at this moment thou art able to love God in thy heart?

The heavens are mine, the earth is mine, the nations are mine: mine are the just, and the sinners are mine: mine are the angels, and the Mother of God; all things are mine, God himself is mine and for me, because Christ is mine and all for me. What dost thou, then, ask for, what dost thou seek for, O my soul? All is thine, all is for thee. Do not take less, nor rest with the crumbs which fall from the table of thy Father. Go forth and exult in thy glory, hide thyself in it, and rejoice, and thou shalt obtain all the desires of thy heart.[41]

---

[41] *Vida y Obras de San Juan de la Cruz*, 1261 (B.A.C., Madrid, 1955). The English translation is that, slightly altered, of David Lewis, *The Living Flame of Love* (London, 1912), 245–50.

CHAPTER V

MERIT, REDEMPTION AND SACRIFICE

> How powerful is suffering when willed as much as sin. He takes no pleasure in bloody sacrifices but much in the presents which his little Son makes to him with all his heart.
>
> —Paul Claudel[1]

UP TO THIS POINT we have considered the dogma of our redemption under what we think is the fundamental aspect for theological analysis, that of vicarious satisfaction. But, since our language proves as usual to be wanting when applied to the divine mystery, our reflections still need to be resumed and completed by further consideration of the aspects of merit, redemption and sacrifice.

---

[1] *L'annonce faite a Marie*, act 3, scene 2; *L'Otage*, act 2, scene 2.

THE OFFERING OF LOVE: MERIT

The Council of Trent, already quoted, leaves no room for doubt: Adam's sin has been forgiven through the merit of Jesus Christ, who has reconciled us to God in his blood. The meritorious cause of our justification is Jesus Christ in his most holy Passion.[2]

The source of merit is charity

Merit implies liberty and also, from the supernatural point of view, charity. But Christ redeemed us freely and for love. Therefore he has merited our salvation.[3]

We may be usefully reminded here of that fundamental principle of moral and spiritual theology already mentioned, that the source of merit is not suffering and difficulty but the love of charity. Times of difficulty and struggle are opportunities for a person to show the promptness and depth of his good will; but this good will flows from charity; consequently, one may carry out an easy task with the same good will, and hence the same merit, as another who carries out a difficult one, simply because he would be equally willing to do what might cost him more.[4] The stronger and more generous love is the better it is able to overcome difficulties, only it is not the difficulty which causes merit but the love. Hence, in order to

---

[2] See Sess. V, cap. 3 and Sess. VI, cap. 7 (Denz. 790 and 799).

[3] Merit presupposes in addition that one is "on the way" (*in via*), that is, on earth. Christ, in so far as he enjoyed the beatific vision, was always "at the destination" (*in termino*) but, until his death on the Cross, he was also on the way there.

[4] See Ia, qu. 95, art. 4, ad 2um. "A less remarkable deed may be more meritorious than a more remarkable deed in so far as a person acts with a more fervent charity" (IIa IIae, qu. 184, art. 8 corp.).

become a soul of great merit it is necessary above all to love much, even in easy matters.

From the moment of his conception in the womb of the Blessed Virgin Mary, the Word Incarnate possessed the virtue of charity and, because of his infused knowledge, the use of his human liberty. From that moment, in fact, he offered himself up for the salvation of mankind with an infinite and, therefore, infinitely meritorious love. "As Christ comes into the world, he says, No sacrifice, no offering was thy demand; thou hast endowed me instead with a body. Thou hast not found any pleasure in burnt sacrifices, in sacrifices for sin. See, then, I said, I am coming to fulfil what is written of me, where the book lies unrolled, to do thy will, O my God. . . . In accordance with this divine will we have been sanctified by an offering made once for all, the body of Jesus Christ" (Heb 10:5, 7, 10).

For Christ, who had come to serve and not to be served, this loving gift of himself for our salvation was the underlying motive of his conscious life. He renewed this offering liturgically at the Last Supper, at the consecration and substantial changing of the bread into his body and the wine into his blood: "This is my blood, of the new testament, shed for many, to the remission of sins" (Matt 26:28). The expression of this redeeming plan culminated in the Passion: "My Father, if it is possible, let this chalice pass me by; only as thy will is, not as mine is" *(Ibid.,* verse 39). And the meaning of his last words before he died is the same: "It is achieved" (John 19:30).

Christ's death is valuable because meritorious and meritorious because suffered with love, the love of the Man-God. St. Thomas comments:

Christ's death may be considered in three ways: first, simply as a death like other human deaths, of which it is said: "Death was never of God's fashioning" (Wis 1:13). But so considered death is due to sin and could not have effected our reconciliation even when suffered by Christ, since "not for God's pleasure does life cease to be" *(ibid.)*.

Secondly, Christ's death may be considered as the handiwork of his murderers, and as such it could not have displeased God more. "You disowned the holy, the just, and asked for the pardon of a murderer, while you killed the author of life" (Acts 3:14). So considered, Christ's death is much more a cause of indignation than of reconciliation.

Thirdly, this death may be considered inasmuch as it is willed by the suffering Christ, who was determined to suffer both because of his obedience to the Father: "He accepted an obedience which brought him to death" (Phil 2:8), and because of his love for men: "the charity which Christ showed us, when he gave himself up on our behalf" (Eph 5:2). This is the reason why Christ's death was meritorious and capable of satisfying for our sins, and why it was so acceptable to God that it sufficed for the reconciliation of all men and even of his murderers.[5]

Christ's merit is infinite in value forever

From the moment of his conception the charity of the Son of God was at its most intense, and enabled him to offer himself immediately and with infinite merit for

---

[5] *Comm. in Rom.* 5, lect. 2, n. 403.

our salvation. It must be emphasized that this charity knew no increase. Christ always merited with the
infinitely valuable merit that is his on great and small
occasions alike, being in a position to repeat unceasingly and with a fervor that could not diminish, "What
I do is always what pleases him" (John 8:29).

The Carmelite theologians of Salamanca summa-
rize this doctrine excellently by explaining that all
Christ's actions together and collectively merited all
that Christ ever merited, but in such a way that he did
not merit anything by one action that he did not merit
by another, and, indeed, by all his remaining actions.[6]

But in that case, when was the work of our redemption accomplished? Was it or was it not accomplished at
the time of his Passion and death? Undoubtedly it was
at this time, and through the shedding of his blood;
only, as St. Thomas observes, this does not mean that
there was any increase in Christ's charity. This charity
was then made manifest in the extremity of his sorrow
and it was precisely through this manifestation that
Christ wished our redemption to be achieved objectively.[7]

What is the reason for this providential plan? It is
that the Passion and death of Christ were especially
appropriate to fulfil the mystery of the redemption in

---

[6] See *Cursus Theologicus*, XVI (ed. Palme), disp. 29, n. 43, 160–1.

[7] See IIIa, qu. 48, art. 1, ad 2um and ad 3um. Our salvation, therefore, was merited by the blood which was shed for us but not
because this *added* to the *perfect* merit Christ possessed already.
See IIIa, qu. 34, art. 3, ad 3um. Christ's humanity, when offered
in the Passion, was sanctified in a new way because it was then a
victim in the act of being offered; but this special sanctification was
due to his charity before the event and to the grace of union which
sanctified him absolutely (IIIa, qu. 22, art. 2, ad 3um).

all its depth, as well as to proclaim its salutary consequences in a concrete form from the mutually complementary and inseparable points of view of justice and mercy. It also gave Christ the opportunity to preach to us by his own example all the virtues, notably perseverance and humility, of which we stand in need. The cross was not simply the gallows from which a condemned man was suspended; it was also, as St. Augustine says, the pulpit from which spoke a Teacher.[8]

Because Christ's infinite love would have been enough of itself and without more ado to secure our redemption, his Passion gives us added reason to marvel at the liberality of his gift. The cross was not necessary for our redemption by the Incarnate Word.[9]

---

[8] See IIIa, qu. 48, art. 1, ad 3um; qu. 46, art. 3 and art. 4: *Comm. in Hebr.* 12, lect. 1, n. 667.

[9] Mgr. Journet writes: "Scheeben rightly observes that Christ could have *merited* grace and glory for us without having to suffer, but *satisfaction* demanded this suffering absolutely; and this because the honor denied God could not be restored to him without estrangement from self, without renunciation and annihilation, while merit, on the other hand, simply demands that one do something for the love of God and to his honor and glory" (*L'Eglise du Verbe Incarne*, II, 214).

We do not think that this argument of Scheeben's can be conceded and we believe that it conflicts with the principles of St. Thomas. Firstly, because of the inverse ratio we have noted in satisfaction between love and suffering (the greater the love, the less the need for suffering), and secondly, because, when we come to consider our Savior's infinite dignity, it seems evident that a single act of love elicited by the child Jesus for our redemption would have possessed of itself the value of superabundant *satisfaction* which was needed for the sins of mankind. The incarnate Word could have made a true satisfaction for us without the least suffering. *In fact* the utmost sorrow accompanied this satisfaction and caused it to appear infinitely deeper and more moving; but we do not think that this suffering was *necessarily* implied in the *satisfaction* of a God-man.

The charity which gave such infinite value to the Passion and death of our Savior preceded both in point of time. The heart of the little child which smiled at Mary and Joseph burned already with the same love that was in the heart of the man dying on Calvary. The cross is the perfect lesson in the gratuitousness of the gift of divine love. There, the shedding of blood was, in the deepest sense of the word, "use-less." But it was this "uselessness" alone which could manifest to the full the mystery of a true love which gives itself unceasingly and without self-interest only in order to give itself yet further. This is its merit, its value and its supreme greatness. God is infinite and God is Love.

Christ is the head of the Mystical Body

Christ merited our salvation as the head of the Mystical Body of which we are the members, a point which is also elucidated by St. Thomas:

> The head and members are as one mystical person, and hence Christ's satisfaction belongs to all the faithful as to his members. In so far as two people are one in charity one of them may satisfy for the other.[10]
>
> Christ possessed grace not merely as a private person but also in so far as he was head of the Church, grace passing, therefore, from him to his members. And hence, also, Christ's deeds stand to him and to us as another man's deeds stand to himself. But it is obvious that whosoever, in a state of grace, suffers for justice's sake merits salvation for himself, as we read in St. Matthew: "Blessed are

---

[10] IIIa, qu. 48, art. 2, ad 1um.

those who suffer persecution in the cause of right"
(5:10). And thus Christ merited salvation not only
for himself but for all his members.[11]

In this way one can better understand the symbolism and efficacy of the Sacrament of Baptism: "Baptism incorporates a man into the Passion and death of
Christ. . . . Christ's Passion is given as a remedy to
every baptized person exactly as though he himself had
suffered and died in sharing it. But Christ's Passion is
satisfaction enough for all the sins of all men and this
is the reason why one who is baptized is freed from all
the punishments due to his sins as though he himself
had made adequate satisfaction for them all."[12]

Vicarious satisfaction supposes that two conditions
be fulfilled. It was precisely this meritorious love of
Christ, the head, which ensured their fulfilment for
his Mystical Body. In the first place, there must be a
solidarity uniting the innocent and the guilty parties
together; secondly, this solidarity must be accepted
by the person offended. This latter condition is obvi-
ously fulfilled since the love uniting us to Christ flows
from the mercy of the Father and cannot but secure his
favor. The solidarity demanded by the first condition
flows from the very nature of love, "the bond which
makes us perfect" (Col 3:14), which unites those who
love one another. The Father, Christ, and ourselves are
made one by love.

---

[11] *Ibid.*, art. 1. Merit follows upon divine grace and charity (Ia IIae,
qu. 114). The incarnate Word "full of grace and truth" (John 1:14),
could win merit *de condigno* (in justice) for all the members of his
Mystical Body. "We have all received something out of his abun-
dance" (John 1:16).

[12] IIIa, qu. 69, art. 2 corp.

BLOOD AS A PRICE: REDEMPTION AND PURCHASE

Redemption

Pause for a moment over the following texts from Scripture:

> You are to be shepherds over that flock which he won for himself at the price of his own blood (Acts 20:28).
>
> A great price was paid to ransom you; glorify God by making your bodies the shrines of his presence (1 Cor 6:20).
>
> A price was paid to redeem you *(ibid.,* 7:23).
>
> What was the ransom that freed you from the vain observances of ancestral tradition? You know well enough that is was not paid in earthly currency, silver or gold; it was paid in the precious blood of Christ: no lamb was ever so pure, so spotless a victim (1 Pet 1:18–19).
>
> Thou, Lord, art worthy to take up the book and break the seals that are on it. Thou wast slain in sacrifice; out of every tribe, every language, every people, every nation thou hast ransomed us with thy blood and given us to God (Rev 5:9).

Holy Scripture, therefore, teaches clearly that Christ has bought us at the price of his blood. Since this is a metaphor the question of its exact interpretation arises and is answered as follows by St. Thomas.

He states that the sinner by his sin hands himself over to a double slavery: on the one hand to that of sin and the devil, and on the other to that of the punishment due to sin. (The obligation to undergo just punishment makes a man a slave in some sense to divine justice in so far as he must then accept that which is contrary to his own will instead of being, as he is by right, the master of his own action and conduct.) But Christ's Passion was superabundant satisfaction for all the faults of mankind as well as for all the punishment due to those faults. Hence it is accurate to say that it accomplished our salvation by way of redemption, liberation and repurchase. By means of it, as though by the payment of a price, we have been released from the double slavery of punishment and sin. The term "price" is justified because it is normally used for all liberating satisfaction, whether liberating from sin or from punishment. So we read in Daniel: "For fault and wrong-doing of thine make amends" (4:24). Christ certainly did not redeem us with money or anything this world thinks valuable, but by giving himself he gave the best it was in his power to give. It is thus that the Passion of Christ is our redemption.[13]

It must be emphasized that St. Thomas shows great circumspection here. One may speak of the Passion, he writes, as of a certain kind of price. Why this reservation?[14] The reason St. Thomas handles the price metaphor with such prudence is that he has in mind the juridical theory of a ransom paid to the devil and wishes to show his disapproval of it.[15] "It was justice in

---

[13] See IIIa, qu. 48, art. 4.

[14] St. Thomas uses what may be called a double attenuation since he says not simply *quoddam pretium*, "a kind of price," but *quasi quoddam pretium*: *as though* the Passion were equivalent to a kind of price.

[15] It would be irrelevant to deal at length here with certain patristic ideas concerning the mystery of redemption. The role of the devil was understood differently according to the juridical, political, and

MERIT, REDEMPTION AND SACRIFICE

relation to God," he writes, "and not to the devil, which required that man be redeemed."[16] "Since redemption was necessary for man's deliverance only as regards God and not as regards the devil, the price was payable not to the devil but to God. And thus Christ is said to have offered his blood, which was the price of our redemption, to God and not to the devil."[17]

The mystery of vicarious satisfaction may be clearly if metaphorically expressed by saying that the price of our redemption has been paid to God by God himself; but it must always be remembered that we are not talking about an act of commutative justice, that

---

poetical theories. In the juridical theory the price of repurchase is to be paid to the devil. In the political theory the devil is the victim of his own abuse of his power against Christ over whom he has no rightful claim. In the poetical theory Christ takes his revenge on the devil.

No one denies that the last two images contain a certain element of truth. As for the first, Richard writes: "The idea of a bargain struck between God and the devil in order to liberate man at the price of Christ's blood has never possessed the consistency of a received theory in Christian antiquity" (L. Richard, *Le Dogme de la Rédemption*, 1932, 104). "A theory generally admitted not so long ago would have it that many of the Fathers of the Church saw in the redemption a bargain between God and the devil. But critical study has reached more prudent conclusions. The fact is that the theory which sought to exploit the image of a ransom, and likened the redemption to a bargain according to the law of commutative justice (Christ being the object of an exchange between God and Satan), reached a dead end. The theory could not but appear inconsistent even to those who framed it, and they were forced to conclude their explanation by escaping from it. It shocked Christian sensibility too much. Nor did it take long to transform it into the less shocking notion, which has been described as 'the abuse of the devil's power." Richard, *Le Dogme de la Rédemption*, 113–15.

[16] IIIa, qu. 48, art. 4, ad 2um.

[17] *L. Richard, Le Dogme de la Rédemption* (1932), 104, 113–115. See *Comm. in Hebr.* 2, lect. 4, n. 141 and 142.

is, about an *exchange*. It is not this aspect of the comparison which should be thrown into relief. Nor is St. Thomas in the wrong, since his insistence on the gratuitous aspect of the redeeming act as an act of loving mercy should be enough to put us on our guard against this particular aberration. All has been forgiven us, all has been given us through the love of our Savior. If we can speak, though not without due discretion and proportion, of Christ's Passion as of a kind of price handed over to release us from the twofold slavery of sin and the punishment due to sin, this is because our liberation was the costly achievement of our Savior's love in shedding his blood for us: "In the Son of God, in his blood, we find the redemption that sets us free from our sins" (Col 1:14). The phrase, "at the cost of his blood," cannot be bettered—so long as it is properly understood.

Fr. Lyonnet's excellent studies, in which he shows the continuity between scriptural and Thomist teaching, are of great service here.[18]

The term, *lutron (αυrpov),* can mean "ransom." There is no reason why St. Paul should not have been inspired by the well-attested Greek custom of emancipating slaves through the payment of a ransom; on the other hand, it is not the emancipation of the Corinthians that he wishes to emphasize so much as "the

---

[18] Especially in *Introduction a la Bible*, II, 859–69; "Conception Paulinienne de la Rédemption," in *Lumiere et Vie,* VII (1958), 35–66; four articles in *Verbum Domini*: "De Notione Salutis in Novo Testamento," 36 (1958) , 3–15; "De Notione Redemptionis," *ibid.,* 129–46; "De Notione Emptionis seu Acquisitionis," *ibid.,* 257–69; "De Notione Expiationis," 37 (1959), 336–52. We offer our thanks to Fr. Lyonnet for allowing us to present several of his conclusions here.

new bonds which attach them to Christ and make them his property. . . ." We have, therefore, for St. Paul, become God's property in virtue of a contract whose every condition has been fulfilled, especially that which the Apostle does not fail to mention, the fact that the price has been paid (1 Cor 6:20; 7:23). But, as Fr. Prat so rightly observes, "the metaphor is not carried too far, and no one intervenes to demand or receive the price." In particular, one is certainly not entitled to conclude from these expressions of St. Paul that he wished to represent the redemption as a kind of commercial barter, in which the jailer refuses to release his prisoner and the vendor his goods save on the condition of losing nothing.[19]

The term, *lutron,* may also mean any instrument of deliverance without there being any question of paying a ransom, and even when this is positively excluded. This usage often occurs in the Judaeo-Greek literature contemporary with Christ,[20] and even more often than not in the New Testament.[21] *Lutron,* therefore, is far from always meaning that a price has been paid.

> Paul goes beyond the juridical notion of punishment. For this does not take into account the attitude of the person condemned and whether he accepts his punishment or revolts against it; in either case justice is assured as soon as he receives

---

[19] Robert et Feuillet, "La soteriologie paulinienne," II, 863–4, quoting Prat, *Théologie de Saint Paul,* II, 230; English translation by J. L. Stoddard, *The Theology of St. Paul,* II (London, 1926), 193, and *Verbum Domini* (1958), 146. St. Thomas and not Scripture speaks explicitly of a price paid to God.

[20] See *Verbum Domini,* 132–4.

[21] See *Ibid.,* 134–8.

it; "justice is done." But for St. Paul and the whole New Testament, on the contrary, Christ's Passion and death only have value through the *voluntary* acceptance of the person who suffers them. . . . What, in fact, St. Paul seems to see above all in Christ's death is the clearest possible proof of the Father's love for men and of Christ's love for his Father—in the form of obedience—and for us.[22] . . . His death and the circumstances of that death were, in reality, the proving, or, if one prefers, the "mediation" of his obedience and love.[23]

This redemption was costly for him since it was the Lamb who was slain who bought men for God at the price of his blood out of every tribe, language, people and nation (Rev 5:9).

Acquisition and redemption

We have already seen (Chapter II, "The Plan of the Redemptive Incarnation") that for both St. Paul and St. Thomas the synthesis of the mystery of the redemption includes the Resurrection and the Ascension. To confine ourselves, therefore, to that aspect of this mystery covered by the metaphorical notion, however legitimate in itself, of a price would be to ignore the complexity of the very term "redemption" itself. Biblical exegesis alone demands a deeper study of the notion of redemption. Fr. Lyonnet writes:

> The New Testament itself points us on towards another idea of redemption and purchase no less

---

[22] *Loc. cit.* in Robert et Feuillet, "La soteriologie paulinienne," II, 880.
[23] *Ibid.*, 881.

familiar to St. Paul than that of the liberation of prisoners and slaves. . . . "Jesus Christ gave himself for us, to ransom us from all our guilt, a people set apart for himself" (Titus 2:14). This is evidently an allusion to the two great events in Israel's history, themselves the "types" *par excellence* of the messianic deliverance: the liberation from the Egyptian slavery and the covenant of Sinai, two events, the memory of which permeates biblical history like a refrain of hope and thanksgiving, and which the Jews delighted to relate together because of their awareness that they were complementary and really formed two aspects, negative and positive as it were, of one and the same mystery.[24]

Just as we find in the Old Testament that the deliverance from the Egyptian slavery is but the first phase of a saving event which culminates in the covenant of Sinai, and that Israel is only delivered from Pharaoh to become the people of God, so the notion of "redemption" has essentially a positive content, indicated by the very etymology of the Latin word (*redimere*). Thus we have the idea of an "acquisition" (*emere*), of a purchase, of a taking of possession by God, who only delivers (*red*) us from slavery to "acquire" us for himself *(emere):* the Pasch and Sinai mutually demand and complement each other. The two notions of "redemption" and "acquisition" are so closely linked in the Jewish mind that each may replace the other.[25]

This is why one finds in the New Testament, side by side with the notion of redemption, as expressed

---

[24] *Ibid.*, 864–5.
[25] *Ibid.*, 866–7.

by the derivatives of *lutron,* that of purchase or repurchase. . . . [The eschatological redemption] will consist, therefore, in the final acquisition of his people by God, when the Son, after triumphing over his last enemy, death, will surrender the kingdom to his Father that God may be all in all (1 Cor 15:25–28). Redemption, then, according to the Latin meaning of the word (and there seems no good reason for changing it to another), means for St. Paul at once "liberation," "purchase," "deliverance," and acquisition; that is to say, as the English word expresses it so exactly, "atonement" or, etymologically, "at-one-ment" in the sense of reconciliation or better still, the reunion of mankind and God.[26]

Christians are not bought by Christ as the slaves of the Gentiles were fictitiously bought by some divinity or other, but rather as the people of Israel was bought by God in order to become, through a covenant sealed with blood, the beloved and exclusive possession of God.

As God saved and bought back for himself in the Old Testament so, also, all proportion guarded, does Christ in the New Testament. Like Yahweh, Christ is proclaimed Judge, King, Spouse, Lord and Shepherd. Jesus is God. Liberation is a positive notion meaning that man becomes the property of God. But Christ achieved our liberation in a way that *cost* him, and this is the new factor, undreamt of in the Old Testament; our purchase was not accomplished without the labors, the

---

[26] *Ibid.,* 867–8.

sweat and the blood of the Son of God.[27]

St. Thomas is a most trustworthy spokesman of the revealed doctrine because he vigorously emphasizes the positive and most important aspect of the mystery of the redemption—as the mystery of man's return to God in the resurrected Christ—and presents more reservedly the metaphor of the price which this return is said to have cost. No justice worthy of the name may accept human blood as the price of an exchange. The divine merciful love alone can light up and transfigure the notion of price and its part in the mystery of our return to God, which was accomplished "at the price of the blood" of the Word Incarnate.

OBLATION AND IMMOLATION: THE SACRIFICE

The theology of sacrifice

St. Thomas' theology of sacrifice is supremely positive. It is dominated by the notion of oblation: all that is ordered in the worship of God may be called a sacrifice;[28] everything, therefore, that is offered to God in order that man's spirit be raised up to him. An important distinction follows from this between the *invisible* sacrifice, by which man offers his spirit to God, and the *visible* sacrifice, which is the sacrament or sacred sensible sign of the invisible sacrifice.[29] There is a visible sacrifice in the fullest meaning of the term when the oblation of something tangible is accompanied by

---

[27] See *Verbum Domini*, 1958, 136–46, and 268–9.
[28] See IIa IIae, qu. 81, art. 4, ad 1um.
[29] See IIIa, qu. 22, art. 2 corp.

an action affecting this thing as it is in itself. An animal, for example, is killed or burnt, bread is broken and eaten.[30] Only it is important to grasp that oblation is not there for the purpose of immolation but, as Durrwell happily puts it, immolation is for the purpose of oblation.[31] It is not a matter of destroying for the sake of destroying, but of honoring God, who is the Lord and Master of *death for life* and not of life for death. Because man is a creature he must acknowledge that everything he has is from God as from his first cause, and that everything must be ordered to God as to his last end. Sacrificial oblations are the symbol of this. Man offers God what he has from God, in order to acknowledge his supreme dominion.[32] If the holocaust is the most perfect sacrifice this is because, as an interior sacrifice, it is no less than the total gift of oneself to God,[33] excellently symbolized by the burning up of a victim, sacrificed out of reverence for the divine majesty and for love of his goodness.[34]

The exterior sacrifice clearly only makes sense in terms of the interior sacrifice of which it is supposed to be both the symbolic sign and the occasion, if not the instrument. Strictly speaking, God has no need of either the blood of goats and bulls or of any visible sacrifice, or, even, of any invisible sacrifice. By reason

---

[30] See IIa IIae, qu. 85, art. 3, ad 3um, and qu. 86, art. 1.
[31] "The study that has been made of ancient religions makes it impossible to see the immolation as a destruction; it was for the purpose of the oblation, forming the negative element in the transfer of a profane thing to divine ownership." F. X. Durrwell, *La resurrection de Jésus, mystere de salut*, 81 (English translation: 61).
[32] See Ia IIae, qu. 102, art. 3 corp.
[33] See IIa IIae, qu. 186.
[34] See Ia IIae, qu. 102.

154

of his infinite transcendence the worship we do him is of no personal use to him *(non proficimus ei)*, but it should, if properly understood, help *us* to make progress in his love *(proficimus in eum)*, and that is why God, for his own glory and our happiness, expects visible and invisible sacrifices of us.[35] It is all at the same time, but in hierarchical order, for his honor and our advantage. This is equally true when we have to make satisfaction for the sins we have committed, since the remission of sin goes hand in hand with the infusion of grace,[36] and there is no satisfaction worthy of God without charity, which, as we have already insisted, is the gift *par excellence* of his mercy.

From the Old to the New Testament

The immediate object of the Old Testament sacrifices was to divert the people from the idolatry to which they were prone; they were to learn to know and reverence the true God by means of sensible signs, and to realize the vanity of any exterior sacrifice which is not the expression of an interior offering of oneself to God. But all these sacrifices were, besides, figures of the sacrifice *par excellence* which is the source of all justification, that of Christ who offered himself on the cross.[37] This is clearly their most interesting aspect for us.[38]

St. Paul teaches that "God has offered his Son to us as a means of reconciliation, in virtue of faith, ransoming us with his blood" (Rom 3:25), and we read in the Epistle to the Hebrews that "unless blood is shed, there

---

[35] *Contra Gentiles,* III, 119.

[36] See Ia IIae, qu. 113, art. 2 corp.

[37] See *Comm. in Psalm.* 50, n. 8, 550. See Ia IIae, qu. 102, art. 3.

[38] See Lyonnet, *art. cit.* in Robert et Feuillet, "La soteriologie paulinienne," II, 869.

can be no remission of sins" (Heb 9:22). In order to grasp firmly the significance of the shedding of blood we should first recall the biblical meaning of expiation, which is also and principally a return to God.

> For the Bible, expiation consists in blotting out sin wherever it is found, that is, first in the people of Israel and then in mankind in general; and since this sin is not thought of simply as a material blot which man himself, therefore, could cause to disappear but is identified with the very rebellion of Israel and of man against God, with what the theologians call the *aversio a Deo*, expiation "blots out" sin precisely by restoring to Israel the presence of God in the midst of his people, by reuniting once again God and man.[39]

It is, however, from this aspect of return to God that the shedding of blood receives an original and positive significance in the sacrifices of the Old Testament. "In Israel, which differs in this from the other religions of the ancient East in which the immolation of the victim takes pride of place, the principal rite is undoubtedly the shedding of blood and is reserved exclusively to the high priest on the feast of Kippur. . . . Nothing could be more dangerous than to take the pagan religions as models."[40] We shall now consider briefly from this point of view the three principal Jewish sacrifices: paschal lamb, covenant and expiation.

---

[39] *Ibid.*
[40] *Ibid.*, 870.

MERIT, REDEMPTION AND SACRIFICE

The blood of the Pasch

In the rite of the first Pasch the blood of the lamb, mentioned twice in Revelation (7:14; 12:11) and once implicitly evoked by St. Paul, is certainly not intended (in the eyes of the biblical writer) to appease Yahweh but to show the exterminating angel which are the houses of those who belong to the people which is Yahweh's first-born son. . . . This is a rite of consecration which separates Israel from the pagan world and already makes her a people apart. Nor does the Bible hesitate to call the paschal ceremony a sacrifice (Exod 12:27), which commemorates the day Yahweh struck the Egyptians and released Israel from a slavery which she came more and more to regard as the very archetype of the slavery of sin (Exod 12:27; Ezek 20:5–9). And Flavius Josephus does, in fact, assure us that, by offering this sacrifice, the children of Israel purified their houses *(Ant. Jud.* 11, 14, n. 312).[41]

The blood of the Covenant

The meaning of the sprinkling with blood in the sacrifice of the Covenant appears even more clearly, if that were possible. Here again immolation is only a preliminary rite carried out by attendants (Exod 24:5); the essential rite of sacrifice is kept for Moses himself and consists in the pouring out of blood upon the altar; then, when the congrega-

---

[41] *Art. cit.* in Robert et Feuillet, "La soteriologie paulinienne," II, 870–1. For Acts 20. 28 and Apoc. 5. 9, see *Verbum Domini*, 1958, 264–5.

tion is occupied for its part in promising to observe the clauses of the Covenant, the sprinkling of the people with blood takes place. As blood, when exchanged between two people in a pact of friendship, "produces a spiritual fellowship between the two parties," so in the sacrifice of the Covenant, concluded in Yahweh's name by Moses, "the blood, which is the soul, is poured over the altar, which represents Yahweh, and the people (that is, over the two contracting parties); thus, through contact with one and the same soul they become one single soul" (Fr. van Imschoot). It is to this sacrifice that Christ explicitly refers when he institutes the Eucharist, on the only occasion in the synoptic gospels when he refers to his blood: "This is my blood, of the new testament" (Mark, Matt), or: "This cup is the new testament, in my blood" (Luke, 1 Cor 11). Hence all references to the Eucharistic blood of Jesus (John 6; 1 Cor. 11), should be referred to this, at least partially, and *a fortiori* those passages where it is stated that the new Israel has become God's people through the blood of Christ (Acts 20:28; Rev 5:9).[42]

The blood of atonement

"St. Paul speaks at least once (Rom 3:25) of the blood of Christ in connection with the sacrifice of atonement. And, in fact, blood played a no less important part there than in the sacrifice of the Covenant."[43]

---

[42] *Art. cit.* in Robert et Feuillet, "La soteriologie paulinienne," II, 871.

[43] *Ibid.*, 871–2.

The sprinkling of blood seven times upon the propitiatory offering was certainly the most important rite. To do this, and for no other reason, the high priest was allowed to enter the Holy of Holies beyond the veil. The purpose of the sprinkling is a purification, a sanctification. "The meaning is clear and again implies a rite of consecration. . . . The Bible teaches once again that, if the Jews attribute this function of purification and consecration to blood, this is because of the life which it contains (Lev 27:11). . . . Life-bearing, identified with life, blood signifies in the Bible an essentially divine reality: it is supremely what consecrates to God, what purifies."[44]

Fr. Lyonnet here observes that the interpretation of the sacrifice of atonement in terms of penal substitution (the victim being immolated instead of the sinner who has deserved to die) is an idea which "seems to have found favor among exegetes since the time of the Reformation in order to support a particular type of theology. . . . There is nothing in the biblical ritual in either Leviticus or Exodus to suggest such an idea."[45]

---

[44] The particular theology which was developed in terms of retributive justice is diametrically opposed to the teaching of St. Thomas concerning the Redeemer himself. In the interests of objectivity, however, it should be remembered that St. Thomas did not exclude the interpretation of penal substitution—though he did not accept it absolutely either (see the context)—for some of the sacrifices of the old Law. "The slaughter of animals signified the destruction of sins, and that man deserved to be killed for his sins; the animals were thus killed in his place to signify the atonement of sins" (Ia IIae, qu. 102, art. 3, ad 5um). Fr. Lyonnet sets this interpretation aside for historical reasons. See Prat, *Théologie de Saint Paul*, 234–5 (English translation: *The Theology of St. Paul*, II, 196–8).

[45] *Art. cit.* in Robert et Feuillet, "La soteriologie paulinienne," II, 873.

The sacrificial victim is always considered as "very holy" in the case of both the sacrifice for sin (Lev 6:18, 22; cf. 10:17) and of the sacrifice of reparation or 'asham (Lev 7:6): that is why it can only be eaten or burnt in a "pure" place (Lev 4:12; 6:19; also Ezek 42:13); it is treated, practically speaking, with a respect which reminds us of that which we show for the Eucharistic species (cf. Lev 6:20–21).[46] The victim whose blood is shed is said to be "for Yahweh" (Lev 16:8–9); it is immolated, "sacrificed," that is to say, according to the biblical idea, it "passes to Yahweh."[47]

---

[46] *Ibid.*, 874. See the fine commentary of Flavius Josephus on the sacrifice of Abraham in Fr. Lyonnet's article noted above in *Lumiere et Vie*, 51, note 49.

[47] *Art. cit.* in Robert et Feuillet, "La soteriologie paulinienne," II, 873. See in the same sense the well-documented article of Fr. Sabourin, "Le Bouc Émissaire, Figure du Christ?" in *Sciences Ecclesiastiques*, II, 45–79 (Montreal, 1959). The author concludes: "There have been two noteworthy attempts to make the scapegoat a figure of Christ. The first had many supporters among ancient writers . . . but to the detriment of the biblical context, since this interpretation inevitably failed to account for data such as the errand to Azazel, the transmission of sins, and, finally, the true and original meaning of the scapegoat. The second attempt, which took place at the time of the Reformation, stays closer to the biblical context but must, on the other hand, adapt itself to a more than suspect formulation of the mystery of our redemption. These two errors, though not equally important, heavily underline the need for a continually alert collaboration between theology and exegesis" (p. 79). Fr. Sabourin puts us on our guard against certain liturgists (he mentions six, see his note 125 on 75) who mistakenly interpret the priest's imposition of hands on the offering at the *Hanc igitur* in terms of the scapegoat; so Beaulieu: "We should remember that at this moment in the Mass we are laying our offences upon the sacred victim who has desired to accept their weight and responsibility" (quoted on 70). Dom Schuster explains the real facts very well: "There is here a preliminary offering and sanctification of the

The scapegoat is another matter altogether. He carries sins and is held to be impure and to contaminate all who approach him. For this reason he is not immolated but driven into the desert, the resort of evil spirits. His blood is not shed. There is no question of sacrifice. "However evocative this 'ancient popular custom' may have been for simple imaginations, it is in fact characteristic of an entirely different rite which everything tends to dissociate from the other sacrifices, especially from sacrifices for sin."[48]

In the last analysis there is no essential difference between the sacrifice of atonement and the sacrifice of the covenant. In one case the blood is primarily intended to establish, in the other to re-establish (for the sacrifice of the Covenant and that of atonement respectively) the union of the chosen people with God. To appease God is at the same time to reconcile man with God, to re-unite him with God.[49] The symbolism of the shedding of blood in the Old Testament would be distorted if one lost sight of the fact that it is above all else positive and leading to union with God in love.

The sacrifice par excellence

"In old days, God spoke to our Fathers in many ways and by many means, through the prophets; now at last

---

oblations intended for the sacrifice; and just as in antiquity every prayer or blessing *super hominem* (over a man) was accompanied by the laying on of hands by the priest, so here in the case of the *oratio super oblata* (the prayer over the offerings) he lays his hands on them" (*Liber Sacramentorum*, II, 82, quoted on 76, note 131).

[48] *Art. cit.* in Robert et Feuillet, "La soteriologie paulinienne," II, especially 896, 897.

[49] See *Comm. in Rom.* 9, lect. 5, n. 803–4. See IIIa, qu. 48, art. 3, and qu. 47, art. 2.

in these times he has spoken to us with a Son to speak for him" (Heb 1:1–2). But the more sublime, simple and brief a word is the more perfect it is. The Word of the Lord clothed in our flesh should be simpler and more efficacious than the words he uttered through the prophets. In fact, the word of the Gospel sums up all the words of the Law. It contains all the precepts of the moral law in the two commandments of love, on which the Law and the prophets depend (Matt 22:40). It includes all the sacrifices, which were offered as figures under the old Law, in one unique and true sacrifice, that of Christ offering himself as a victim for our salvation (Eph 5:2).[50]

The Son of God is the greatest of all the gifts made by God to a mankind ruined by sin. Therefore, also, the most splendid of sacrifices is that in which Christ offers himself as a sacrifice breathing out fragrance. All the sacrifices of the old Law were offered to prefigure this unique and perfect sacrifice. All the figurative details of the sacrifices of the old Law must be interpreted in the light of the true sacrifice which is Christ's.[51]

"The blood of bulls and goats, the ashes of a heifer sprinkled over men defiled, have power to hallow them for every purpose of outward purification; and shall not the blood of Christ, who offered himself, through the Holy Ghost, as a victim unblemished in God's sight, purify our consciences, and set them free from lifeless observances, to serve the living God?" (Heb 9:13–14). It is indeed through his own blood that the Son of God has accomplished the eternal redemption of our souls and bodies, and St. Thomas here notes that the Apos-

---

[50] See Ia IIae, qu. 102, art. 3. See IIIa, qu. 48, art. 3 corp.
[51] See *Comm. in Hebr.* 9, lect. 3, n. 442, 444.

tle explains and justifies the efficacy of Christ's blood under three heads. We should, he says, consider *who* shed this blood, *why* and *how* he shed it.

The person to whom this blood belongs is the Son of God himself. Hence it is evident that his blood is purifying: "He is to save his people from their sins" (Matt 1:21).

The reason why Christ shed his blood is to be found in the Holy Spirit, who prompted Christ to redeem us for the love of God and of his neighbor. "He shall come as a violent stream, which the spirit of the Lord driveth on" (Isa 59:19, Douay); but the Spirit is purifying: "The Lord shall wash away the filth of the daughters of Sion, and shall wash away the blood of Jerusalem out of the midst thereof, by the spirit of judgment, and by the spirit of burning" (Isa 4:4, Douay). Therefore the Apostle says: "He offered himself through the Holy Ghost" (Heb 9:14), and speaks of "that charity which Christ showed to us, when he gave himself up on our behalf, as a sacrifice breathing out fragrance as he offered it to God" (Eph 5:2).

Christ cannot but be immaculate: "What can be made clean by the unclean?" (Eccl 34:4, Douay).[52]

---

[52] See IIIa, qu. 22, art. 1, art. 2. "Christ's Passion was the offering of a sacrifice insofar as Christ suffered death of his own free will and for love; but insofar as he suffered at the hands of his persecutors, his Passion was not a sacrifice but the gravest of sins" (IIIa, qu. 47, art. 4, ad 2um). "Christ's Passion was a grave evil on the part of his executioners; but it was a sacrifice on his part because of the charity with which he suffered. It is Christ who is said to have offered the sacrifice, not his executioners" (IIIa, qu. 48, art. 3, ad 3um). "Christ's charity during his suffering was greater than the malice of those who crucified him" (*ibid.*, art. 2, ad 2um). See also IIIa, qu. 49, art. 4, ad 3um.

Christ did not commit suicide but was killed by the Jews, and yet

Because he offers *himself* Christ is both the high priest and the victim of his sacrifice.[53]

The immolation of Christ crucified combines together on a higher plane both the holocaust of expiation and the sacrifice of the covenant. This was the sacrifice of the high priest according to the order of Melchizedek,[54] the sacrifice of the Lamb of God.[55]

Behold the Lamb of God

The historical reason for the paschal supper was that it commemorated the liberation of the Jews from the Egyptian slavery. The prophetical reason for it was that it prefigured Christ's immolation.[56]

Two lambs were immolated every day in the Temple, one in the morning and one in the evening. The sacrifice of lambs was unchanging; it was the most important and dominated the rest. It was a figure of

---

Christ died voluntarily. How? The Jews were guilty of this homicide (which was in fact a deicide) because they did all that was necessary to kill the Savior. Christ could have resisted had he so desired, and since he did not so desire he died voluntarily although killed by the Jews (see *Compendium Theologiae*, 230, n. 485).

[53] See IIIa, qu. 22, art. 2, art. 3.

[54] See *ibid.*, art. 3, ad 3um; art. 6. Christ's priesthood was prefigured by the Levitical priesthood in so far as it was a sacrifice offered through the shedding of blood. It was prefigured by the priesthood of Melchizedek for two reasons, one being that this priesthood was superior to the Levitical priesthood (Abraham paid tithes to Melchizedek), and the other, that Melchizedek offered bread and wine. But bread and wine signify the unity of the Church, which is the fruit of Christ's priesthood, and it is under the appearances of bread and wine that Christ's sacrifice is communicated to the faithful.

[55] See Boismard, "Le Christ Agneau, Redempteur des Hommes," in *Lumiere et Vie*, quoted above, 91–104.

[56] See Ia IIae, qu. 102, art. 5, ad 2um. See *Comm. in 1 Cor. 5*, lect. 2, n. 246.

the sacrifice *par excellence* which is that of Christ.

Christ is called the Lamb of God because of his two natures, one human the other divine. It is in virtue of his divine nature that his sacrifice is capable of making atonement and satisfaction, since "God was in Christ, reconciling the world to himself" (2 Cor 5:19); but it was in virtue of his human nature that Christ could offer himself as a victim.

Christ is called the Lamb of God as much as to say, the Lamb offered by God, that is, by Christ himself who is God. He is also called the Lamb of God, meaning the Lamb of God the Father, since it is the Father who empowered him to make such an offering of himself as a victim for the sins of the world. When Isaac asked Abraham: "Where is the lamb we need for a victim?" Abraham replied: "God will see to it that there is a lamb to be sacrificed" (Gen 22:7–8). "God did not even spare his own Son, but gave him up for us all" (Rom 8:32).

Christ is called a lamb first of all because of his purity: "It must be a male yearling lamb . . . that you choose, with no blemish on it" (Exod 12:5). "The ransom that freed you . . . was not paid in earthly currency, silver or gold" (1 Pet 1:18). Secondly, because of his meekness: "He shall be dumb as a lamb before his shearer" (Isa 53:7, Douay). Thirdly, because of the benefits he brings us, and first of all, clothing: "Lambs are for thy clothing" (Prov 27:26, Douay); which the Epistle to the Romans explains: "Arm yourselves with the Lord Jesus Christ" (13:14); secondly, food: "And now, what is this bread which I am to give? It is my flesh, given for the life of the world" (John 6:52).

> This Lamb "takes away the sin of the world," that is, causes it to disappear. Under the Law the blood of bulls, goats and lambs could not do this (Heb 10:4), but the Lamb of God "pardons all iniquity" (Hos 14:3). "So, on the cross, his own body took the weight of our sins" (1 Pet 2:24). "Our weakness, it was he who carried the weight of it, our miseries, and it was he who bore them" (Isa 53:4). As the gloss says, the author here writes *the sin* and not *the sins,* in order to show clearly that our Lord takes away every kind of sin. "He in his own person, is the atonement made for our sins" (1 John 2:2).[57]

The Lamb of God is one of the dominating figures in St. John's Revelation. Need we be surprised? Christ's sacrifice was offered with bloodshed once only, on the cross, but its consummation lasts eternally. Although the saints in heaven have no further need of atonement, they must always continue to receive their fulfilment from him on whom their joy and glory depend.[58]

---

[57] *Comm. in Joan.* 1, lect. 14, n. 257–9.
[58] See IIIa, qu. 22, art. 5.

IN THE LOVE OF GOD AND THE PATIENCE OF CHRIST[1]

CHRIST IS THE SUN OF JUSTICE (MAL 4:2), he is the origin and crown of our faith (Heb 12:2). But if we are to be saved we must share in the merit of his Passion and death. He who is not reborn in Christ cannot be justified, for a man is only just to the extent that he partakes in the merits of our Savior's Passion.[2]

---

[1] "May the love of God and the patience of Christ show you the way" (2 Thess 3:5).

[2] See Council of Trent, Sess. VI, Proem, and chaps. 2, 3 and 7 (Denz. 792, 794, 795, 800). Justification is the change from the state of original sin to that of adopted children of God through the reception of Baptism. Baptism of desire, that is, the implicit or explicit wish for Baptism, may act for baptism by water. The seven sacraments owe their efficacy to the incarnate Word (IIIa, qu. 60 prol.), and are *par excellence*, and each in its own way, the sensible signs and instruments of redeeming grace. The Sacrament of sacraments is the Eucharist, which is both sacrifice and sacrament, and

167

"God was in Christ reconciling the world to himself" (2 Cor 5:19). We entreat you in Christ's name—that is, for the love of Christ, writes St. Thomas—make your peace with God. But if God has already reconciled us to himself, why should we do it again? Everything has been done. Certainly we owe our reconciliation with God to God himself, but if we are to gain by it we must make our own contribution; we must win merit."[3] Salvation is a personal matter.

By the cooperation of their faith and deeds the justified may grow in perfection and be further justified (Jas 2:22). The Church asks for this growth in justice (that is, holiness) in her prayer: "Grant us, Almighty God, an increase of faith, hope and charity."[4] The practice of the three theological virtues enables us to share in the riches of the redemption, with regret for our faults, filial abandonment to God's Providence and confidence in his mercy, and all in virtue of love.

It would be a sign of sinful self-deceit to neglect works of satisfaction for our sins such as fasting, almsgiving, prayer and the works of mercy,[5] but "the greatest evidence we can give of our love and so make satisfaction is to accept patiently the trials and pains of this life in union with Jesus Christ."[6] What matters most,

---

is especially associated with the grace of theological charity. The last anointing is like another baptism in that, *of itself*, it disposes the faithful for immediate entry into the joy of God the instant death occurs (*Contra Gentiles*, 4, 73). Besides the sacraments we may also gain indulgences.

[3] See *Comm. in 2 Cor.* 5, lect. 5, n. 200.
[4] Prayer at Mass for the Twelfth Sunday after Pentecost, quoted by the Council of Trent, Sess. VI, cap. 10 (Denz. 803).
[5] See *Ibid.*, cap. 14, and cap. 3 (Denz. 807, 913).
[6] *Ibid.*, Sess. XIV, cap. 9 (Denz. 906). See *The Imitation of Christ*, bk 3, chap. 18–20. It would be a mistake to think that the sacramental

in order to make satisfaction and purify oneself, is that these works of atonement and this patience in time of trial should be the fruit of a sincere love and thus bear witness to one's good will. "Above all things, preserve constant charity among yourselves; charity draws the veil over a multitude of sins" (1 Pet 4:8). "Bear the burden of one another's failings; then you will be fulfilling the law of Christ" (Gal 6:2).

The more pure and generous love is the less attention does it pay to its own meritoriousness and the more it places all its confidence in the infinite mercy which is the source of every gift and all forgiveness.[7] And as love grows in this confidence the need for punishment or pain in making satisfaction decreases. "You see, Mother, even if I had committed every possible crime, I should still have the same confidence, I should still feel that this multitude of sins was like a drop of

---

penance given us by our confessor always remits all the temporal punishment due to our sins (*ibid.*, Sess. VI, cap. 14; Sess. XIV, cap. 8; Denz. 807, 905).

[7] As St. Thomas notes, it is also because of justice that God is ready to forgive sins. "The forgiveness of sins is called commiseration (*miseratio*) since it springs from and is the work of divine mercy: but we may also see justice in this forgiveness since 'all the ways of the Lord are mercy and truth' (Psalm 24:10, Douay). We may apply this to God in so far as, when he forgives sins, he does something worthy of God (in *quantum remittendo peccata facit quod Deum decet*); as St. Anselm says: 'You are just when you spare sinners, for this is truly worthy of you'; and we read: 'Deliver me in thy justice'" (Psalm 30:1, Douay). (*De Veritate*, qu. 28, art. 1, ad 8um.)

And St. Thérèse of Lisieux writes in the same sense: "I hope for as much from the good God's justice as from his mercy; because he 'is compassionate and merciful, long-suffering and plenteous in mercy'" (Psalm 102:8). *Lettres*, Lisieux, 1948, 392. English translation: F. J. Sheed, *The Collected Letters of St. Thérèse of Lisieux* (London, 1949), 291.

water thrown into a burning brazier. You will soon be telling the story of the converted woman who was a sinner, and who died of love. Souls will understand it at once; this example will encourage them."[8]

Salvation is personal and meritorious, but it is not simply a private matter for each one; it involves the community as a whole. There is no room for individuals in the body of Christ. No one can win merit or be saved without helping to save his brethren. The more a soul advances in holiness, the more, not only purifying, but redemptive do its sufferings become. Besides the gift of faith in Christ another gift has been made to us: that of being able to suffer in union with him for the salvation of the world (Phil 1:29).

> "I am glad of my sufferings on your behalf as, in this mortal frame of mine, I help to pay off the debt which the afflictions of Christ still leave to be paid, for the sake of his body, the Church" (Col 1:24). Not that we are to jump to the conclusion that our Savior's satisfaction was, objectively speaking, insufficient—Christ's blood was enough to redeem any number of worlds—but Christ is a single Mystical Body, of which he is the head and we the members, and God, in his wisdom, disposes the merits and the sufferings of each and all, of the head as of the members. Christ's merits are infinite, and each member has that degree of merit which corresponds with his vocation as one of God's children. There is nothing lacking in the afflictions of Christ, but for love Paul must bear in his flesh some

---

[8] St. Teresa of Lisieux, "Novissima Verba," July 11th. The sinner in question went straight to heaven.

share of personal affliction and so share in the merits of the Redeemer *for the building up of the Mystical Body.* Christ must suffer in Paul, his member,
as he does in all his members. All the saints have
suffered, are suffering and will suffer thus for the
Church until the end of time.[9]

I should never have thought it possible to suffer so much! Never, never! I can only explain it to
myself by the burning desire that I have had to save
souls.[10]

The spirituality of St. Teresa of the Child Jesus is
in perfect harmony with the dogmatic teaching of St.
Thomas Aquinas.

. . . I realize that we aren't all made alike; souls have
got to fall into different groups, so that all God's
perfections may be honored severally. Only for me
his infinite mercy is the quality that stands out
in my life, and when I contemplate and adore his
other perfections, it's against this background of
mercy all the time. They all seem to have a dazzling
outline of love; even God's justice, and perhaps his
justice more than any other attribute of his, seems
to have love for its setting.[11]

On the 9th of June this year, the feast of the
Holy Trinity, I was given the grace to see more
clearly than ever how love is what our Lord really
wants. I was thinking about the souls who offer
themselves as victims to the divine justice, with the

---

[9] See *Comm. in Col.* 1, lect. 6, n. 61.
[10] *Novissima Verba*, September 30th, the day of her death.
[11] *Manuscrits Autobiographiques*, A, folio 83 verso. English translation: R. A. Knox, "Autobiography of a Saint," (London, 1958), 219.

idea of turning aside and bringing upon themselves the punishments decreed against sinners. I felt that this kind of self-immolation was a fine gesture, a generous gesture, but it wasn't at all the one I wanted to make.[12] The cry of my heart was something different: "My God, why should only your justice claim victims; why should there be no victims of your merciful Love? Everywhere that Love is misunderstood and thrust on one side; the hearts upon which you are ready to lavish it turn away towards creatures instead, as if happiness could be found in such miserable attachments as that; they won't throw themselves into your arms and accept the gift of your infinite Love. Must this rejected Love of yours remain shut up in your own Heart? If only you could find souls ready to offer themselves as victims to be burnt up in the fire of your love, surely you would lose no time in satisfying their desire; you would find a welcome outlet, in this way, for the pent-up force of that infinite tenderness which is yours. . . ."

Ever since that memorable day, love seems to pierce me through and wrap me round, merciful love which makes a new creature of me, purifies my soul and leaves no trace of sin there, till all my fear of Purgatory is lost. To be sure, no merits of my own could even win me entrance there; it is only for the souls of the redeemed. But at the same time I felt confident that the fire of love can sanctify

---

[12] St. Thérèse understood perfectly that one could only offer oneself as a victim in this way through love, and that in such a case one would be more aptly described as the victim of loving justice than simply of justice. In this St. Thérèse joins hands with St. Thomas' profoundest intuition concerning the redemption.

us more surely than those fires of expiation; why
should he inspire me with this ambition to become
a victim, if he doesn't mean to satisfy it?[13]

"To live in an act of perfect love I OFFER
MYSELF AS A BURNT-OFFERING TO YOUR
MERCIFUL LOVE, calling upon You to consume
me at every instant, while You let the floods of
infinite tenderness pent up within You flow into my
soul, so that I may become Martyr to Your Love, O
my God! . . . When that martyrdom has prepared
me to appear before You, may it cause me to die,
and may my soul hurl itself in that instant into the
eternal embrace of *Your merciful Love.*"[14]

[13] *Manuscrits Autobiographiques,* A, folio 84 recto and verso (*Autobiography of a Saint,* 219–21).
[14] *Ibid.,* "Acte d'offrande a l'Amour misericordieux" (*Collected Letters,* 330–1).

SELECT
BIBLIOGRAPHY

AQUINAS, Saint Thomas. *Summa Theologiae*. ed. The Aquinas Institute. Green Bay, WI; Steubenville, OH: Aquinas Institute; Emmaus Academic, 2018.

DURRWELL, F. X., C.SS.R. *The Resurrection*. London and New York: Sheed & Ward, 1960.

HENRY, A. M., O.P. (Editor). *Theology Library*, volume 2. Cork: Mercier Press, and Chicago: Fides, 1957.

JOHN OF THE CROSS, St. *The Complete Works of St. John of the Cross*. Translated and edited by E. Allison Peers, 3 volumes. London: Burns & Oates, and Westminster, MD: Newman Press, 1953.

JOURNET, Charles. *Church of the Word Incarnate*. London and New York: Sheed & Ward, 1955.

KNOX, R. A. *St. Paul's Gospel*. London and New York: Sheed & Ward, 1956.

PRAT, Fernand. *The Theology of St. Paul*. London: Burns & Oates, and Westminster, MD: Newman Press, 1958.

PETIT, Francis, O.Praem. *The Problem of Evil*. New York: Hawthorn Books, 1959. Pontifex, Dom Mark. *Providence and Freedom* (American edition, *Freedom and Providence*. New York: Hawthorn Books, 1960).

RAHNER, Karl, S.J. *Theological Investigations*, volume 1. London: Darton, Longman & Todd, and Baltimore: Helicon, 1961.

SCHEEBEN, Matthias J. *Mysteries of Christianity*. Steubenville: Emmaus Academic, 2021.

SMITH, G. D. (Editor). *The Teaching of the Catholic Church*. London: Burns & Oates, and New York: Macmillan, 1947.

TAILLE, M. de la, S.J. *The Mystery of Faith*, 2 volumes. London and New York: Sheed & Ward, 1950.

TERESA OF JESUS, St. *The Complete Works of St. Teresa of Jesus*. Edited and translated by E. Allison Peers. London and New York: Sheed & Ward, 1946.

THERESE OF LISIEUX. *The Story of a Soul: The Autobiography of the Little Flower*. Charlotte: TAN Books, 2010.